CHALLENGED PARENTING

A practical handbook for parents of children with handicaps

BONNIE WHEELER

Regal Books

A Division of GL Publications
Ventura, CA U.S.A.

The foreign language publishing of all Regal books is under the direction of GLINT. GLINT provides financial and technical help for the adaptation, translation and publishing of books for millions of people worldwide. For information regarding translation, contact: GLINT, P.O. Box 6688, Ventura, California 93006.

Published by Regal Books
A Division of GL Publications
Ventura, California 93006
Printed in U.S.A.

Library of Congress Cataloging in Publication Data
Wheeler, Bonnie.
    Challenged parenting.

    1. Parenting.   2. Handicapped children—Family Relationships.
3. Cerebral palsied children—Care and treatment.   I. Title.
HQ773.6.W47   1982   649'.151   82-18144
ISBN 0-8307-0835-9

To Georgiana Walker,
mentor and friend

ACKNOWLEDGMENTS

Thank you, God, for:

each of the parents who shared with such honesty the heartaches and joys of challenged parenting;

Dennis for his love and support;

Susan Dunlap for her perseverance as reader and reactor;

and my editors: Don Pugh for his godly patience and encouragement and Laurie Leslie for her diligence and enthusiasm.

CONTENTS

INTRODUCTION

I have called you by name; you are mine. When you go through deep waters and great trouble I will be with you. When you go through rivers of difficulty, you will not drown! When you walk through the fire of oppression you will not be burned up—the flames will not consume you. For I am the Lord your God, your Savior, the Holy One of Israel, *Isaiah 43:1-3.*

"Please sit down, Mrs. Wheeler. I've suspected this for some time. Now I'm certain. Your daughter has *cerebral palsy!*"

I was shocked. Stunned. Numb. And, for the next few years, very lonely. We saw an orthopedist, a neurologist, an opthamologist, and a pediatrician. We belonged to a church, had friends and a loving (though far away) family. There were always people around.

And still I felt alone.

I didn't have the foggiest idea where to go for help and answers. Our pastor thought cerebral palsy was terminal and I ended up consoling *him*; the doctors never looked beyond their specialty to see the whole child; friends and family were more perplexed than we were. And we were all puzzled and uncertain about dealing with this *new* situation. New because at three-and-a-half our daughter had acquired a label.

I called a few organizations, read Dale Evans's *Angel Unaware* (the only book on handicaps I could find at the time), continued seeing all the doctors, and tried to explain the unexplainable to a child.

There seemed to be so little help that after awhile I stopped looking. And we continued on—alone. Or so I thought. We weren't alone—just uninformed.

Our introduction into the world of challenged children didn't end with our daughter's diagnosis. Our second child, a few months before his fourth birthday, had a severe head injury that almost took his life and left him very hyperactive. Our third child was threatened with numerous surgeries by his second birthday and spent four years wearing leg braces like his sister's.

At this point I felt completely overwhelmed and sought comfort at a neighborhood church. One evening during a communion service my husband, Dennis, accepted Jesus as his personal Saviour and I recommitted my life to Him. God started showing us immediately that the experiences with our first three children had been His training and preparation for a new ministry and He guided us into adoption. (More on this in *Of Braces and Blessings*, Christian Herald Books.)

We specifically requested a little girl with cerebral palsy, and nine months later three-year-old Becky joined our family. Seven months later fifteen-month-old Benji (also diagnosed as having cerebral palsy) arrived, and a few years later Melissa, a deaf-blind victim of maternal rubella, rounded out our family.

By 1974, when we adopted Becky, many things had changed from the day I was given Julie's diagnosis. I had a smidgen more confidence, there were more organizations dealing with families affected by cerebral palsy, and more information was available. And *this* time I had a social worker and a public health nurse guiding me through the maze of parenting a challenged child.

I started learning that we were definitely not alone; other parents were going through this often painful training process. Every year in the United States 200,000 babies are born with birth defects and thousands more are handicapped through accidents and illness. There are approximately fifteen million Americans whose daily lives are affected in some way by birth defects.

By the 1978-79 school year, it was estimated that there would be well over seven million handicapped Americans under the age of twenty-one.

I definitely wasn't alone. With Becky we became very much a part of a group effort.

When I started working on this book I wanted to reflect that feeling of empathy and solidarity that I had gained from other parents of challenged children. I sent out numerous questionnaires to parents, pastors, doctors, therapists, and teachers; I will gratefully use their input.

This book is prayerfully planned to lead you through your earliest fears that something is wrong with your child, through the diagnosis and acceptance of the fact, into the daily practicalities of rearing the child with a handicap, and into eventual celebration as that child reaches his/her fullest potential.

This book has a three-fold purpose: (1) to help parents of challenged children on their journey; (2) to be used by pastors, educators and doctors as a reference and resource; and (3) to be read by friends, relatives, and caring people who want to understand and help us—parent and child—on our journey.

Occasionally I use examples of our family. I'm by no means holding us up as a picture of perfection (or even near perfection!). I make no pretense of having found all the answers, no claim to all the solutions. Our family's journey isn't over yet, but we no longer travel alone.

There are many words used to *label* our children: crippled, handicapped, disabled—more recently, special and exceptional. The first three words bring to mind negative images and each word connotes limits. Special and exceptional are more positive but still set the children apart.

Last year on a telethon the host used the term *challenged children*. I liked the sound of it. I saw mental pictures of winners and overcomers and I went to the dictionary to look up the definition of challenge: "Anything as a demanding task that calls for special effort or dedication." That definition seems so very appropriate in our situation where much special effort is required from our children and much special dedication is required from us.

Challenged children. Challenged parenting.

Part I

CHALLENGED PARENTING—THE PSYCHOLOGY

A PRAYER FOR PARENTS OF CHALLENGED CHILDREN
from 1 Corinthians 13:4-7

LOVE IS PATIENT AND KIND. Oh, Lord, we need your patience so much as we live with slow bodies, slow minds.

LOVE IS NEVER JEALOUS OR ENVIOUS—not even when my neighbor's child gets an A+, wins another tennis trophy, not even then.

LOVE IS NEVER BOASTFUL OR PROUD. Help me not to brag unduly to my friend whose child will never walk.

LOVE IS NEVER HAUGHTY. Some days I convince myself that I'm special just because you've entrusted me with this child.

LOVE IS NEVER SELFISH—even when it means pushing my child on to new steps, even when the pushing hurts me most.

LOVE IS NEVER RUDE. This is a hard one, Lord, as people glare, stare, and call my child names.

LOVE DOES NOT DEMAND ITS OWN WAY. Help me to remember that a sweet spirit making a request will often gain more for my child than harsh demands.

LOVE IS NOT IRRITABLE OR TOUCHY. Forgive me, Lord, but I so often am.

LOVE DOES NOT HOLD GRUDGES AND WILL HARDLY NOTICE WHEN OTHERS DO IT WRONG—Aunt Susie's concern for the "family line," that insensitive doctor last week, that little girl next door who calls my child, "the cripple"—strike them from my memory, Lord.

LOVE IS NEVER GLAD ABOUT INJUSTICES. For just a minute, Lord, I was glad their child was sick. "Maybe now they'll understand a little of what we go through every day of our lives"; forgive me, Lord.

IF YOU LOVE SOMEONE YOU WILL BE LOYAL TO HIM NO MATTER WHAT THE COST—no matter how many nights' sleep I lose to rub aching muscles, no matter how many doctors' bills we pay, no matter how many friends I lose, or meetings I miss, no matter . . .

YOU WILL ALWAYS BELIEVE IN HIM. Oh, yes, Lord! My child will live, my child will love and serve you. Oh, yes, Lord!

ALWAYS EXPECT THE BEST OF HIM—the very best my child is able.

ALWAYS STAND YOUR GROUND IN DEFENDING HIM. Just as you are our heavenly advocate, Lord, help me defend this precious child in a world that often doesn't understand or care.

NOW ALL THAT I KNOW IS HAZY AND BLURRED. There are so many unanswered questions, Lord. Grant me patience and trust until that someday when I will see "things clearly."

UNTIL THEN THERE ARE THREE THINGS I HOLD ONTO:
Faith in your sovereign will,
Hope in my child's potential,
and love.

Chapter 1

THE EARLY YEARS

Yet what we suffer now is nothing compared to the glory he will give us later, *Romans 8:18.*

Lean back, close your eyes. Picture Adam and Eve strolling hand-in-hand through the garden of Eden. Adam plucks a flower, hands it to Eve and begins weaving a dream: "We'll have a boy this first time—"

Eve coyly interjects, "He'll look just like you, dear."

Adam continues, "I'll teach him about the animals I named. Why, I bet he'll run faster than the gazelle."

"And have the curiosity of a monkey," Eve giggles.

They smile at each other and plan on. Earth's first parents dreaming earth's first dream of a perfect child.

Keep your eyes closed and remember the movie *Carousel*. Can you hear Billy Bigelow singing his poignant soliloquy, "My Boy Bill"?

Picture most expectant parents fondly dreaming of a baby. Their baby. Images of "perfect," "better than me," "a chip off the old block" come to mind.

I close my eyes and remember when I was expecting our first child. I dreamed of a perfect child that would embody all the qualities and character traits I lacked; do all the deeds I had never done.

Far too often our ego and self-worth are inseparably wrapped up in our children. We dream and then brag about our children's grades, piano virtuosity, or sports prowess as if we had done it all. (We even brag about the date of baby's first tooth!)

Our children reflect us, and when that reflection is impaired so is our ego. Sadly, the problem isn't the child who bears the brunt of it all, but a society that demands and expects beauty, strength, and perfection.

Shattered Dreams

The dream of superbaby is threatened the very first time we suspect something is "just not quite right." Most of us experience those suspicions for weeks or months: a baby that doesn't roll over or sit up on schedule; a child that seemingly "ignores" loud noises; that haunting feeling that something just isn't right.

After trying to ignore our suspicions we take the child to our doctors with fear and trembling. And more often than not the doctors refuse to take our concerns seriously. "Now, Mrs. Smith, you're not to worry. No two children progress the same." If the unfortunate parent was a first timer, "You first-time mothers just worry too much."

After the doctor's reassurances we go home—not really reassured, and now feeling strangely guilty for ever having doubted our own child's abilities and potential.

When finally the fears and suspicions cannot be stifled any longer we grow more insistent and often change doctors.

We each receive the diagnosis and confirmation of

our fears at varying times, since approximately half of all birth defects are detected at birth. Some birth defects such as cleft palate and missing limbs are immediately obvious at birth; Down's syndrome is usually confirmed by blood tests. Others of us wait for agonizing, frustrating months or years before we get a definite diagnosis.

For some, the diagnosis is never clear-cut. A diagnosis should define the problem, but some children defy definition and fit in the cracks. For many of us the diagnosis will only be as good as the tests given and the person interpreting them.

Those of us who wait for a diagnosis must still cope eventually with the pain of confirmed fears and altered dreams. Yet often those very fears have prepared us and we experience some measure of relief:

"At least I know I wasn't crazy!"

"Mike's diagnosis of cerebral palsy at age five made it easier to care for him because we realized we had been putting unfair expectations on him."

"Thank you, Lord. Now I know what I can do to help."

Beginning the Journey

The earlier we learn of our child's challenge the greater our shock, since there has been little or no preparation. (This same shock happens when a child is suddenly struck by accident or illness.) But even when the shock is most severe, God is able to bless and comfort. Barbara shares her story:

"At my baby shower, someone gave me a copy of Dale Evans's *Spiritual Diary*. When I was leaving for the hospital to give birth I tossed it in my suitcase at the last minute. After Danny's birth the doctor came in on Tuesday to tell me that our sixth child was a Down's syndrome baby.

"In my pain I turned to the Tuesday reading and there

was a prayer written by Dale Evans after the birth of her daughter Robin. 'Thank you, God, for giving me a Mongoloid child because it has brought me closer to the cross of calvary.'

"God gave me an answer right away that Danny was *His* child. When I shared the prayer with my husband we marveled that this book, with that prayer for that particular Tuesday, was in my hands when I needed it most!"

We owe it to our children and ourselves to get the best, most accurate possible diagnosis, and we often have to shop around for this. There is a delicate balance—a balance between getting the best possible diagnosis and not wasting our lives in a vain search for the diagnosis we *want* to hear.

We need to use the diagnosis as a tool. A tool to get the proper care, treatment, therapy, and schooling for our children. We have to be extremely cautious not to let ourselves be crippled by the very diagnosis the doctors place on our children. Our daughter was no different after the doctor told us she had cerebral palsy, yet I went into a tailspin and eventually became a firm believer that labels belong on jars not kids! We also need to realize that labels are to be convenient tools not absolute truths.[1]

Our fears and suspicions have now been confirmed. Our dreams have been shattered or altered. Down through the centuries parents have dreamed of the "perfect" child, yet we know that Christ was the only perfect One. Now we have to start accepting the fact that our dream child never existed and never would have! Most parents come to this realization at some point in their lives. The realization is just forced on parents of challenged children sooner.[2]

Like anyone who has suffered a loss or death, we must proceed to work our way through the next part of our journey before we can help our children. The dream is changed, altered, gone.

Mourning begins.

Chapter 2

THE MOURNING PROCESS

To everything there is a season, and a time to
every purpose under the heaven:. . . a time to
mourn, *Ecclesiastes 3:1,4, KJV.*

The day I learned that our daughter's three-and-a-
half-year orthopedic problem was cerebral palsy—a *permanent condition*, not a *temporary problem*—my
mourning process began. Mourning all those unreal
expectations, mourning the prospect of an uncertain
future. Mourning the death of a dream.

In all my studying, reading, sharing with other parents
and professionals, this mourning process appears as a
necessary but painful step towards accepting reality,
eventual healing, and ultimately helping our children
reach their fullest potentials.

Mourning is a normal, biblical process—a *passage*,
not a permanent stopping place. As typical as the process
is, the rate we each travel through it is *atypical* and there

can be days, months, or—sadly—years between stage stops. Occasionally some of us run into trouble when we get caught up at one stop and can't make it on through to the final destination.

There are five commonly recognized steps in the mourning process: denial, anger, guilt, despair, and acceptance.

Denial Stage

Many parents flatly refuse to accept the diagnosis at first: "He's just slow." "We'll see another doctor." "Not *my* child!" This stage helps us delay reality until we can better cope.

I was numb during my denial period. I had worried for so long when none of the special shoes and braces worked. I couldn't deny the diagnosis itself; instead, I retreated into numbness and tried to deny my feelings.

In many of the questionnaire responses I noticed that the fathers and grandparents seemed to spend more time at this stage stop than the mothers. My theory is that we mothers usually have had our fearful suspicions for awhile, and since we're primarily responsible for the care of the child we're almost forced to face reality and move on to the next stages.

There are two major and potentially tragic dangers in this denial stage. The first is that one of the family might deny not just the diagnosis but the child. How often have we heard or said, "My child is deaf" or a similar phrase? Yet I can't remember ever hearing a child introduced as, "My child is pneumonia." We need to learn to separate our children from his/her diagnosis, remembering that *the diagnosis defines the problem not the child*. We need to say, "My child has a hearing loss."

The second danger of denial is that in denying the diagnosis our children will miss out on needed therapy and treatment while we keep insisting the problem doesn't exist. Peg Rankin comments on denial: "In order to overcome our problems, we need to face reality head-on. If we are in trouble, let's admit it. Ignoring it will not make it go away."[3]

Anger Stage
My head throbs, my jaw tightens, my fists clench, and my stomach is in knots. Anger.

We get angry at the doctor whose misfortune it was to have to tell us that our perfect child—isn't.

We get angry at children who stare.

Angry at ourselves: "If I hadn't _____ this would never have happened."

Angry at our spouse: "If you hadn't _____ this would never have happened."

Those of us who have to wait for a diagnosis express anger at the months or years that are wasted when an earlier diagnosis could have led us to earlier treatment.

And then as any child cries out to its parent, we cry out our anger to God. Well-meaning people then warn us that we must never be angry with God. Professionals warn us that anger must be dealt with and that—once again—ignoring the problem won't make it go away.

Jim Conway's daughter lost a leg from cancer and people warned him, "Don't say those things about God. God will be angry with you if you talk that way about Him." Conway refutes this: "We need to realize that God is able to defend Himself. He can handle whatever an anguished person dishes out and His self-image won't be destroyed."[4]

We need to take our anger to God. Be honest with Him, then ask Him to take the anger away so it doesn't harm our relationship with Him.

Despair Stage
During the initial shock and denial the numbness

blunts some of our pain. During the despair-depression time we hurt—oh, how we hurt! Despair is a natural reaction to our unfulfilled expectations, and now we have to change those expectations.[5]

Despair is a necessary part of the mourning process; it is also the easiest to give in to. This is the point where we really need to get help and talk to someone we can trust: a pastor, doctor, or friend. Find a parent support group, start one if you have to, but don't give in to the quicksand of despair.

Trinia's initial reaction to her daughter's hearing loss was a broken heart. "I was devastated that she would never hear God's bird sing, or a bubbling brook, or sound of horses' hooves."

Centuries ago, the psalmist recognized this despair, "The Lord is close to those whose hearts are breaking" (Ps. 34:18).

Guilt Stage

Before we can move on through to peace and acceptance we invariably bump into guilt. Guilt is actually defined as "the state or fact of having committed a crime, legal offense, or wrongdoing." Giving birth to a challenged child doesn't fit any of those categories; yet we so often assume responsibility, and subsequently guilt, for something over which we had little or no control.

Where denial is often the hardest stage for fathers to work through, guilt most often traps mothers. "I carried this child in my body, therefore," we reason, "I'm responsible—guilty!"

On the questionnaire responses, most of the mothers had their round with guilt. Causes ranged from a reasonable "Was it my running?" to the irrational "Was it because her initials are M.R.?" to the poignant "I was a carrier of a genetic disease."

Lisa Blumberg, a challenged adult, tells about the

guilt that burdened her mother and concludes, "No parent has reason to feel guilty about a child's disability unless the disability stems directly from neglect or abuse. Guilt about a child's disability is an unnecessary burden. It can only make the lives of both parent and child miserable."[6]

As Christians, even if child abuse or neglect was the cause, we need to remember that Christ died for our sins and, yes, He can forgive *even that*.

I'm now addressing the parents who had no control over what happened to their child but who are still loaded with guilt. That guilt can be more crippling and damaging to us than anything that can strike our children's bodies.

Recognize the guilt for what it is and don't let it overwhelm you. We need to get all the available information on our child's challenge. Often just logically finding out the cause, or probable cause, will help alleviate our guilt. We need to discuss our guilt-causing concerns openly with our doctors and ask for material and resources to read. When we received our daughter's diagnosis one of my first reactions was, "What could I have done to prevent this?" I went back to the doctor just to talk, taking a list of questions with me. At the end of that question-and-answer session I believed that there really was nothing I could have done to prevent my daughter's cerebral palsy.

We need to talk to our pastors. Explain our feelings and ask for helpful Scripture. We need to talk to God and turn the guilt over to Him.

Other parents share their advice:

"There will always be guilt and 'what-ifs,' but I realized there was nothing I caused or could have prevented."

"An adequate diagnosis helped relieve my guilt as I realized it was nothing I caused or could have prevented."

"The guilt (I was in a car accident and had x-rays)

didn't last long as we all dearly loved Danny."

"I realized my guilt was a reaction to a shattered dream of a child who'll never run or play ball."

"Sure I felt guilt! My sister lost two babies with the same thing. I was a carrier. Sometimes I still feel guilty but not always and not so often. When it comes I give it to God and tell Satan, 'Get lost! I don't need that!' "

And wise words from another mother, "I have guilt but I refuse to sink in it because it can do no good. I pray about it as it comes. Each day I realize more and more how completely Jesus took my guilt to the cross with Him so I need not feel guilty. I don't want the guilt and Jesus is happy to reassure me that *He did indeed take it all for me!*"

Acceptance and Peace Stage

We each at our own pace travel through the mourning process as we let the child of our mind die and move on to letting the real child live.[7]

As a Christian, it strikes me as ironic that we spend so much time mourning our child's imperfections when we *know* that the only perfect one—ever!—is Jesus. Our prayer needs to be, *"Lord, help me to see beyond my child's limits and imperfections as you see, so patiently, beyond mine."*

Norm Wright, marriage counselor, author, and father of a mentally challenged son, shared his point of acceptance in an interview. "One of the things I had to work through was the acceptance of the fact that I was the father of a son, but would never really know what that experience was like."[8]

Other parents share:

"My child isn't perfect; no one is."

"The shock lasted a few days and then I knew it was time to go to work."

"I went through three phases: I accepted my child;

then I asked what can I do for my child and then asked, what can I do for other children?"

Chapter 3

QUESTIONING

As He was walking along, he saw a man blind from birth. "Master," his disciples asked him, "*why* was this man born blind?" *John 9:1,2.*

I didn't include questioning with the mourning process, although many professionals include it with anger. Mourning is a process with a beginning and an end. Questioning is not just a once-passed-through stop, but a continuing part of life.

My natural, cowardly inclination is to avoid this chapter. Christians more learned than I have written volumes on the whys of suffering and trials, but I believe I can't continue without acknowledging the whys, the questioning we all go through.

As I've researched the why of my "whys" I've come across a variety of conflicting answers. I barely get my questions sorted out and find an almost satisfactory answer when a new situation comes up and there I go again.

Why God?
Why me?
Why us?
Why our child?

I've read books and heard speakers warn me not to question God and I'll resolve to ask no more questions. Then a new situation comes up and instinctively up pops another question: *Why, God? Why?*

Why God? Why?

There are many different medical reasons for challenged children: genetic, illness to the mother during pregnancy, trauma at birth, illness or accident to the child after birth.

Only 20 percent of birth defects are traceable to primarily hereditary factors; 20 percent are due to something in the environment of the baby that affects it while developing inside the mother. The majority of defects is caused by an interaction of hereditary and environmental factors.[9]

One doctor explained that our daughter was turned wrong at birth and her oxygen supply was temporarily cut off during birthing. *At last*, I thought, *I have an answer*. Then the doctor added, "but at best this is just an educated guess."

I thought I had sorted out my questions and arrived at a simplistic answer—"it's God's will"—when we adopted Becky. For two months I drove to Children's Hospital for her weekly therapy. I saw a newborn with her spine open; a beautiful golden-haired angel with perfect vision and cerebral palsy so severe that he couldn't hold his eyes open. I saw a handsome teenage athlete stand upright for the first time since the amputation of his cancerous leg. He cried out in pain. So did I. There was a black boy—well, really only half black; fire had burned

half the black away and left his hands immobilized with
scar tissue.

I who had dared think, *I understand. I have an
answer . . .* cried out again, "Why, God? Why?"

I read yet another book that warned against questioning God. *That author is much better educated than I am*,
I reasoned. *I must be wrong.* Finally in my confusion at
the world's answers I took my questions to the Lord.

Job questioned.

He suffered the loss of everything he held dear and
he asked, "Why didn't I die at birth?"

"Why should light and life be given to those in misery
and bitterness who long for death, and it won't come?"

"Why is a man allowed to be born if God is only
going to give him a hopeless life of uselessness and frustration?"

Yet even while questioning God, Job trusted:
"Though he slay me, yet will I trust in him" (Job 13:15,
KJV). And while God never directly answered Job's
questions, He did eventually return to Job more than was
taken.

John the Baptist questioned. "Are you really the Mes-
siah?" he asked. Jesus was not embarrassed. He was not
even particularly concerned. This question did not take
Him by surprise, it did not shock Him. He did not even
raise His voice (that ought to suggest something to us
about whether or not the Lord will raise His voice to us if
we express our doubts to Him).[10]

The disciples questioned. "As he was walking along
he saw a man blind from birth. 'Master,' his disciples
asked him, 'Why was this man born blind? Was it a result
of his own sins or those of his parents?'

" 'Neither,' Jesus answered. *'But to demonstrate the
power of God'* " (John 9:1-3, italics added).

As if we don't have enough questions of our own
there are those of "Job's comforters," such as, "How can

this happen to a Christian family? If you only had more faith!"

Philip Yancey tells us that "if God halted all tragedies which involved Christians it would insulate us from complete identification with the world and the world needs to see us struggling as they do—living out the principles proving that God's grace is sufficient."[11]

And to those who dare question our faith there is Psalm 23:4, "Yea, though I *walk* through the valley . . .," and Isaiah 43:2,3, "*When* you go through deep waters and great trouble, I will be with you. *When* you go through rivers of difficulty, you will not drown! *When* you walk through the fire of oppression, you will not be burned up—the flames will not consume you. For I am the Lord your God, your Savior, the Holy One of Israel" (italics added).

In all of these reassurances He says *when*, not *if*. No promises that we'll avoid the flood, fires, and troubles of life. No guarantee that by being Christians we can avoid all of that. Nothing that says that "becoming a Christian equips us with a germ-free, hermetically sealed spacesuit to protect us from the dangers of earth."[12]

But He does give us promise after promise that He will walk with us. He will uphold us.

In her book *A Step Further*, quadraplegic Joni Eareckson relates a reason for suffering, "It demonstrates His ability to maintain the loyalty of His people even when they face difficult trials. If being a Christian brought us nothing but ease and comfort the world wouldn't learn anything impressive about our God."[13]

The father of a cerebral palsy child shares his view: "We certainly do not know the reasons why but that too is part of the life of faith, trusting even when we can't understand at all."[14]

In trying to sort out the whys of challenged children, I've come to believe that God is a God of order. He created the universe with certain natural laws: laws of cause and effect. As man has interfered with those laws through sin it has resulted in drug abuse, disease, polluted environment. And through those consequences have come birth defects.

The psalmist says, "You made all the delicate inner parts of my body, and knit them together in my mother's womb. . . . You were there while I was being formed in utter seclusion" (Ps. 139:13,15).

God knows when a child will have a missing limb, He sees the twisted body. He sees and knows but chooses not to change things. He doesn't change the way the baby is forming, but He does prepare and enable us to cope—to ultimately triumph.

In that same way God knew His own Son would suffer great agony. He didn't step in and change things (and as a loving parent I'm sure He must have wanted to), but He did prepare His Son. Prepared Him not only to endure but to triumph!

And He prepares us.

"Why Not a Miracle?"

As Christians, somewhere along the line—or constantly—we pray for our child's healing. A miracle. Well-meaning people also urge us to pray for a miraculous healing and then question our faith when the miracle doesn't arrive.

(Having just fought our way out of the grips of guilt about our child's initial diagnosis we definitely don't need this.)

Unbelievers say there are no miracles and they don't pray. And occasionally we Christians pray and don't act. We need to pray for a miracle, keep praying, and never stop praying. And act.

When the Israelites were standing at the Red Sea with the waters before them and the army behind them they desperately prayed for deliverance. Finally God commanded, "Quit praying and get the people moving! Forward, march!" (Exod. 14:15)

They had to *act* and step forward before God performed the miracle and parted the seas. So we need to step forward and act, even as we are praying. We need to use the various resources for our children that God provides. Talk to the experts. Use the therapist and doctor's skill. And keep praying.

Author Peg Rankin writes, "Just as God is sovereign in whom He heals, He is also sovereign in the methods He employs. He can heal with medicine or without medicine, gradually or instantaneously."[15]

In our family we have seen this in action as God has worked His miracles in varying degrees and ways. Julie was a slow, gradual miracle. She had a slight curvature of the spine and a 3/4-inch leg length difference. She had years of braces and corrective shoes. Julie graduates from high school this year with *no* sign of cerebral palsy. She's just finished her third year of varsity volleyball! A slow miracle, but for cerebral palsy definitely a miracle.

Becky has had many surgeries, years of therapy, different bracing. She is still very involved. *But* she is mainstreamed into our neighborhood school, on the honor roll, and walking. At each stage where Becky surpasses the doctor's prognosis she's an *ongoing* miracle.

Benji's prognosis was negatively confirmed by several doctors: cerebral palsy and retardation. At fifteen months he was just starting to sit up. Didn't walk or talk. And we were cautioned that he probably never would. We prayed for Benji's miracle. At eighteen months he was extensively tested and was on age level in *everything*. Today he is a top student with not a trace of cerebral palsy. God blessed us with three months of *daily miracles*.

Joni Eareckson confirms author Rankin's view of

healing: "Here is the conclusion I've come to regarding miraculous healing: God certainly can, and sometimes does, heal people in a miraculous way today. But the Bible does *not* teach that He will *always* heal those who come to Him in faith. He sovereignly reserves the right to heal or not heal as He sees fit."[16]

Vicky's little girl has a rare disease that is always fatal by age one. Now that Toria is eight years old her doctors shake their heads in mystification, "but she can't be alive!"

Toria is in a wheelchair, can't walk at all; but she's alive and happy and loves Jesus. She is also confident, "Jesus promised me that one day I will walk!" Toria is patiently content to wait for the rest of her miracle. Virginia Escher wrote as she was dying from cancer, "Some say that God gets glory through miraculous healings, but how much greater is the glory that God brings to Himself by sustaining His child in the midst of suffering."[17] At the tender age of eight, Toria has learned the secret of that sustaining grace.

Melissa has been in our family four years. She is now twelve. We prayed that she would receive her miracle like our other children have. She has made some progress in the past few years, but she is still deaf. Still blind. In her case we are trusting the Lord for daily strength and wisdom. He has given us the assurance that when Melissa goes home to heaven she will *see* Jesus in all His glory and *hear* the angels sing. Isn't that perhaps the greatest miracle of them all?

Guidelines in Questioning

Edith Schaeffer says, "We are meant to find in the word of God a balance in our understanding of affliction but will never end up (at least not in this life) with a precise, mathematical explanation of why."[18]

I have learned, through my years of questioning,

some guidelines to keep me in check:

1. While I can question I must not demand answers and accountability from God.

2. I must be willing to wait (maybe until heaven) for my answers.

3. I must not let my unanswered questions cause bitterness and come between me and the Lord.

4. I must remember and apply the Serenity Prayer to my questioning: "God grant me the courage to change the things I can [my attitude]; the patience to accept the things I cannot change [my child's diagnosis, waiting for answers]; *and the wisdom to know the difference*."

Philip Yancey tells about looking ahead instead of dwelling on the past: "The emphasis I see in the Bible is not to look backward and find out if God is responsible in order to accuse Him. In answering Job, God completely ignored that issue. The emphasis is rather on looking ahead to what God can make out of seeming tragedy."[19]

Two more children and six years after my questions at Children's Hospital I complacently thought I had progressed some—I was even working on this book! Then I stood beside Becky's hospital bed. She had just had surgery on both hips, both legs, and both feet. Her legs had pins and wires and were casted. If this surgery wasn't successful I knew she would be back for more surgery within the year. She cried out in pain and I echoed her cries, "Why, God? Why does this one child have to suffer so? Do you know what it's like to watch while your child suffers???"

As I stood there with my unanswered questions and tearstained face I heard in reply John 3:16, "For God so loved the world, that he gave his only begotten Son . . ."

As I watched Becky writhing in pain and heard that verse I could see Christ, God's only Son, writhing in pain much worse than Becky's, while His Father looked on. And I knew that instant that God understood my suffering parent's heart, and I realized that as long as I'm an imperfect being, still "seeing everything through a glass darkly" I'll have questions.

And standing by our daughter's hospital bed I asked once more, *"How can this be used for our good and God's glory?"*

Chapter 4

COPING

For I can do everything God asks me to with the help of Christ who gives me the strength and power, *Philippians 4:13*.

In raising a "normal" child (if such a child exists!) there are scores of books, magazines, speakers, experts, friends, relatives, our own experiences, and centuries of cultural experience to help and guide us. Few of us have had the experience of being handicapped ourselves and there is no cultural tradition to tell us how to raise our children.[20]

When we have no previous experiences to draw on, no cultural experience to help and guide us, when we are daily forced to face our insufficiencies, where can we turn? In my experience, God uses our challenged children to keep me turned towards Him. When I run head-first into my inabilities, He takes over.

For twelve years we lived in a large metropolitan area.

During those years I slowly and carefully built up a network of resources—doctors, teachers, therapists—who knew our children and their specific, special needs. Then we moved to a small rural area community and I had to start all over.

Uncountable times when I have gotten frustrated at my inability and the overall lack of information (especially with the multi-challenged Melissa), I exhaust myself running around in circles trying to find help and answers. Then I finally cry out my helplessness to God.

Time after time, God has given me a common sense solution, put me in touch with just the right person, or given me the holy patience to wait for an answer. I'm gently reminded of 2 Corinthians 3:5: "Not that we are sufficient of ourselves to think anything as of ourselves but our sufficiency is of God" (*KJV*).

God always values our availability more than our ability, and this is the secret of being able to cope, and cope triumphantly! as challenged parents.

Thank you, Lord, for this challenge. I confess my inability and humbly give you my availability to parent this precious child. Help me become, with copious amounts of your enabling, the parent you want me to be.

Ready for New Responsibilities

We've received the diagnosis, worked our way through the mourning process, and questioned. We've given up certain dreams and expectations and asked for God's enabling. Now we are ready for new responsibilities. It is time to claim God's promises for strength and joy and get on with life, with raising our children, with coping.

Victor Frankl wrote of life in a German concentration camp, "Everything can be taken away but one thing:. . . to choose one's attitude in any given set of circumstances."[21]

Several mothers expressed their decisions to cope:

"There's no time to sit and feel sorry for ourselves. We have to try. We have to know in our hearts that we tried."

"Our goal is to help our son reach his fullest potential, whatever it may be. For us to do the best we can and enjoy life together, the good and the bad, and take it one day at a time."

"I knew that as much as I loved my daughter, God loved her even more. I needed to do all I could and leave everything up to Him."

"We realized that since there was nothing we could do to change the situation we had to deal with it."

"Remember you can't handle it all, you're not God. But He is with you and will always listen."

When we reach this stage and make the choice to cope, when we stop asking, "Why me?" and start asking, "How can I help my child?" then we are accepting our child and our challenge. The most challenging, sometimes frustrating, but infinitely rewarding experience of a lifetime is beginning.

With our first three children I stumbled through my on-the-job training and we all, surprisingly, made it. When we applied to adopt another challenged child our youngest was not yet five. I was starting to feel insecure about this forthcoming new commitment and I signed up for a *basic parenting class* offered at a local hospital.

The class ran for six weeks and was taught by various pediatricians. It covered everything from new babies to older children with learning problems. Most of the information I already knew, but it was a good refresher and helped my self-confidence.

My husband and I took a first-aid class together. While this should be *basic* for everyone, it is *essential* for parents of challenged children, considering the extra frequency of illness and accidents they have.

Those two classes helped my self-confidence at a time when it needed all the bolstering it could get. My only regret was that I hadn't taken the classes earlier.

Without adequate information and counseling we can get so caught up in trying to find solutions and answers on our own that we can't do our best job of parenting.

To cope we need *help and information*—information that I didn't have with our first child and was determined to find with our fourth. What follows is by no means a comprehensive guide to resources but it is a starting point.

1. Talk to your doctors. Ask questions. If they don't have the answers you need, ask them to refer you to a resource that can give you the needed information.

2. Talk to your pastor.

3. Get out your telephone directory. (Each community will have different listings.) I used a California Bay Area phone directory; you'll have to do some extra searching if your listing differs from mine. I first turn to the index at the back of the Yellow Pages and look up *handicaps*. Under that is a listing for *Social Services and Welfare Organizations*. Since several of our children have cerebral palsy, I'll look up resources available under that listing.

Under Social Services I find: Easter Seal Society; March of Dimes; Regional Center; United Way; United Cerebral Palsy. A call to the local United Cerebral Palsy office gets me an information booklet, a counselor, a parent support group.

A call to the local Regional Center tells me that they help parents of developmentally disabled persons use essential public and private services. They sent me a brochure listing all their services—information and referral, counseling, diagnosis and evaluation, lifelong planning, respite care, guardianship, financial assistance for necessary services.

Under state listings (white pages) I find: Crippled Children's Services (now California Children's Services). They offer financial assistance for necessary services and medical appliances.

Under county listings I find the county health department. They work with CCS and we had a county public health nurse that helped us with our CCS services. She attended clinic appointments with me, made home visits, and was a jewel at helping me sort out red tape.

Under the listing for schools I find a school for the orthopedically handicapped. The staff of these schools usually are very up on current resources and patiently answered questions.

4. Find a parent support group! I can't stress this enough. All the parents that I have talked and shared with tell how important these are. Those who didn't have a group available started their own. There was one at the school Becky went to, one through the Regional Center, another through United Cerebral Palsy. We chose the one at Becky's school because it was closest.

At one meeting the highly trained psychologist who led our group asked what had been most helpful. We unanimously answered, "just being able to share honestly with people who understand."

Once I had made contacts I was notified (either officially or by other parents) about lectures, seminars, classes, and books that were helpful.

All of this—and more—was available to help me cope with parenting Becky, not because she was adopted but because she had cerebral palsy.

When you start calling around don't get discouraged and give up as I originally did. If that first contact doesn't get you the desired information, keep calling. The key is persistence.

His Sufficiency

Some of the mistakes I made with our first child were due to my insecurity, and I'm sure our daughter picked up on that. With Becky I was better read, better educated, and more self-assured. That positiveness reflected back to her. Our job requires special dedication and we owe it to ourselves and our children to utilize every possible resource.

As I daily cope with challenged parenting I daily run up against my limitations. But I have an extra resource, one that Paul told about in 2 Corinthians 12:9,10: "[Jesus] said, 'But I am with you; that is all you need. My power shows up best in weak people.' Now I am glad to boast about how weak I am; I am glad to be a living demonstration of Christ's power, instead of showing off my own power and abilities."

Chapter 5

IMAGE MAKERS—IMAGE BREAKERS

So God created man in his own image, in the image of God . . . *Genesis 1:27, KJV.*

I am certain we parents realize our importance to the healthy mental and physical development of our children. Everywhere we turn there is another expert pointing out that importance:

"When Daddy says, 'you are a terrible little boy,' the child doesn't question his father's credentials, he questions only his own worth as a person."[22]

"The child's picture of himself is formed largely out of the image which they [parents] reflect back to him. They are like a mirror from which he derives his own sense of worth and value."[23]

Bruce Narramore reechoes this, "His [the child's] only mirror is the comments and evaluations he receives from others. So the next ingredient of the young child's self-esteem is the input he receives from the persons who are always nearby, his parents."[24]

Read any material on developing healthy self-esteem in children (healthy, strong, bright children). Reread the same material with your challenged child in mind. If our role in helping our other children develop healthy self-images is important, then it is essential with our challenged children. When our challenged children look at us and play, "mirror, mirror," what are they seeing, feeling, and hearing reflected from us? Unconditional love and total acceptance? Or impatience, fatigue, frustration?

Our job is essential and difficult right from the start. Our challenged children are often preemies that stay in the hospital weeks or months after the mother is released. When that happens they miss some of the important bonding every baby needs.

Our children might have twisted, spastic, or paralyzed limbs. Others have cleft palates, blind eyes, or slow minds. From day one, these children require more medical care than our other children, and it is so easy for us to fall in the trap of substituting our medical duties for the hugs and cuddles they need.

This problem snuck up on me after Becky's last surgery. I had to give her a bed bath, lift her off and on the bedpan, do some physical therapy, bring her meals to her, help her with her schoolwork (and take care of a big house and five other children). One night I went to tuck her in and I realized all I had done that day was *take care* of her; I had gotten too busy and too tired to *just care*.

Adding to the other complications, our challenged child is usually our very first experience with a child with special needs. We are often just plain scared. Scared our child will break, scared we will hurt him, scared we will do something wrong.

These children often have "equipment" that complicates spontaneous hugs and cuddles. Once we are aware of this we can be creative and give our challenged children all the cuddles, love pats, eye contact, and verbal reassurances we humanly can.

Before we can help our children with their self-esteem we need to honestly (and without guilt) examine our feelings and reactions. The first time I had to do something for one of our children and felt squeamish about it I was overwhelmed with guilt, "But this is my child, I can't feel this way!"

I'm not a trained nurse and much of this doesn't come easy for me. I have a queasy stomach and fight nausea at the sight of blood. Yet, I have doctored ugly pressure sores from leg braces, emptied more bed pans than some hospital nurses, and taken care of Melissa's monthly menstrual needs. I have held Becky's hand while the doctors removed pins and wires from her legs (Daddy watched, I didn't!). I've cleaned up more urine, feces, vomit, and blood than I care to remember (in fact, I'm starting to feel woozy now!). There have been times when I go to God and yell out, "I can't! This is gross! Help me . . ." He's been there *every* time.

We need to take inventory of our feelings before the Lord (an understanding parents group can be helpful here too):

1. Do I see my child as a blessing or a burden?
2. Are my feelings positive or negative?
3. What negative feelings do I have? (List them.)
4. Try to analyze their cause (without feeling guilty).
5. Take the negatives to the Lord and plead for His healing of your inner responses.
6. *Forgive me, Lord, for ever seeing this child as anything less than the blessing you intended her for. Heal my inner fears and reservations. Take away my subconscious negativeness that can possibly reflect back to my child. Thank you for your sufficiency.*

When we feel positive we will reflect that back to our children. When we feel negative, no matter how limited our children are, they will pick that up. When we can work our way through the process and honestly see our children as a blessing and not a curse, as part of God's perfect plan for us and not some divine punishment or random genetic accident, as a joy—then we will be able to help our children develop positive, healthy egos. Only when our children see our love and respect can they learn to love and respect themselves.

Building Positive Images

Those fortunate children who have bright minds and strong, healthy bodies can take a lot of guff from us at home and go to neighborhood schools, scout and athletic activities and get enough positive feedback to help them develop some healthy self-esteem.

On the other hand, our challenged children go out into a world that often, at best, tolerates them, at worst, rejects them. There will be some days when we will be their only source of comfort and positive reflection.

We can spend our lives getting the world's best medical treatment to help our children reach their fullest physical and mental potential and it will all be wasted, vain effort, if they end up with straight bodies, productive minds, and twisted, crippled self-images.

George W. Paterson stresses that "the handicapped child must discover that his disability does not cancel out or even reduce his essential worth as a person. He needs to learn that human dignity and value do not depend on 'normality' but that he is a person of worth and significance, handicap and all."[25]

In *The Unexpected Minority* the authors emphasize this: "What makes the handicapped 'special' are the attitudes and reactions of others who are not handicapped, and the greatest harm to the handicapped child or adult stems from this socially engendered impairment of daily life, self-concept and future—not from the functional impairments themselves."[26]

I have seen this happen to Becky. After her recent surgery and six weeks in casts, she started physical therapy. She started walking again ahead of schedule. All the feedback she got from us, from her therapists, and from her physician was very positive. She was months ahead of schedule and just as proud as could be. Then she went to the park with some other children: "You can't do this," "Better slow down for Becky," "This isn't safe for you." She saw herself through their eyes, retreated to her wheelchair and came home in tears.

"If one thing is clear from autobiographies of the handicapped, it is that the first hazard many face is the demoralization that can result from having one's competence as an individual constantly challenged while one is growing up—not because one is incompetent but because the able bodied *think* one is."[27]

It's a tragic self-fulfilling prophecy, like the little ditty:
I'm not what I think I am; I'm not what you think I am;
But I am what I think you think I am.

Our self-image is influenced by other people's values, and a negative self-concept can develop when we accept the values of other people instead of the values of God.

We have the exciting job of helping our children see and accept God's value system. To help them see not as the world sees, or their mirrors reflect, but as God sees.

"For the Lord seeth not as man seeth; for man looketh on the outward appearance, but the Lord looketh on the heart" (1 Sam. 16:7, *KJV*).

The world does everything it can to make our job tougher—billboards, magazines, and TV screens screaming out messages for more sex appeal, the "beautiful people"; millions of dollars are spent advertising a distorted value system.

Bill Gothard talks of self-image and warns that if we fail to comprehend God's values and purposes for the way we are made that we will eventually develop self-rejection and an unconscious bitterness towards God for making us the way He did.

Gothard uses the analogy of a picture frame that is appropriate for the child who has a noticeable challenge. "Our outward appearance is only a frame around the inward qualities that God wants us to develop. Focus on the picture, not the frame." He continues to relate that our appearance is *logical* when God has specific achievements He wants to accomplish.[28]

I thought of the thousands of lives that have been blessed by Joni Eareckson in her wheelchair, Ken Medema with his blindness, and Merill Womach with his burn-scarred face. Thousands of lives touched, souls saved, because those three special people refused to accept the world's value system and allowed God to use them.

I'm convinced that helping our challenged children establish a personal relationship with Jesus, giving them our unconditional love, and helping them develop a positive self-image are the most important legacies we can give them.

When Becky joined our family she was three-and-a-half years old. She had never been to church or Sunday School. We were her fifth placement in her short lifetime. That first week in Sunday School she was like a dry, thirsty little sponge as she listened to stories about Jesus. Here was someone who loved unconditionally: *No matter what color my skin is, no matter how my legs look, no matter . . . Jesus loves me.* She realized that no matter how many more moves were in her future, no matter how many more operations were ahead, she had found a constant, someone who never changed, whose love never changed. That simple, basic knowledge told to a three-year-old brought tremendous healing to her battered little ego.

Building Self-Image

Becky's cerebral palsy limits her somewhat physically, but how she sees her challenge and herself will minimize or maximize her ultimate potential and the impact of this challenge on her life. We've stressed to all of our children the importance of the adage, "It's not what you have but what you [and God] do with it."

We have shared with Becky many times that her sitting up, walking, and being an honor student are all miracles from God—all things the doctors said would never happen.

Becky has no illusions about her cerebral palsy, yet most of her perception is positive. She accepts that she will *probably* never (we *never* say *never* at our house!) rollerskate or ride a two-wheeler. She concentrates on her strong points—her very bright mind—and maximizes her potential. After her recent surgery she missed four weeks of school, had a tutor five hours a week and still made the honor roll. We were thrilled; she was upset about the two Bs!

Bruce Narramore says, "Our self-concept is the source of our personal happiness or lack of it. It establishes the boundaries of our accomplishment and defines the limits of our fulfillment. If we think positively about ourselves we are free to achieve our true potential."[29]

I hope you can handle one more Becky story because this one illustrates Dr. Narramore's point. Becky's casts had just been removed and her therapist was trying to get her to stand for the first time in seven weeks. Becky was as weak and wobbly as a newborn colt. "Doctor said it's gonna be slow and for me not to expect any miracles." Becky tried to stand, grimaced with pain, and kept talking, "But he just doesn't know me and God!"

We live in a rambling Victorian house with dozens of stairs, and under normal circumstances none of our children has any trouble navigating them. After Becky's surgery I had to carry her to the bathroom, down to the family room, up to bed . . . and I have a weak back. There were days when I would carry her downstairs and we would have to wait for Daddy to come home to take her back upstairs.

Becky knew that the lifting and carrying was hurting my back and it started bothering her. I couldn't deny that carrying her was hurting my back, and to give her a nice, adult speech—"Yes, dear, my back is hurting, but it's not your fault"—just wouldn't have made it.

I prayed for wisdom, expecting some wise answer. Instead the Lord had me use a dumb joke, "I'm Becky's thirty-seven-year-old mother with a ninety-year-old back." Becky thought it was hilarious (nine-year-olds laugh at anything!) and delighted in telling all her visitors about "my silly mother who has old parts." It also helped her see that we all have challenges of some sort.

When I asked other parents about building positive self-images in their children they responded:

"Positive input essential!"

"You be proud of yourself, your family, and especially your special child."

"Our child has a positive self-image because we feed her very positive thoughts about herself."

"We always talk about our child in a way that puts her in the best possible light."

Dr. C. Everett Koop gives us all a positive goal to work towards: "It has been my constant experience that disability and unhappiness do not go hand-in-hand. There is remarkable joy and happiness in the lives of most handicapped children. Some have borne burdens I would have found difficult to face. But I know what can be accomplished by rehabilitation of the child. I know these children become loved and loving, that they are creative, that their entrance into a family can be an extraordinarily positive experience."[30]

That experience becomes even more beautiful as we show our children God's unconditional love reflected through their families; as we watch them develop positive self-esteem; and as we nurture their strength and will to not only meet their challenge but be overcomers.

NOTES PART I

1. Joan McNamara and Bernard McNamara, *The Special Child Handbook* (New York: Hawthorn Books, Inc., 1977), p. 52.
2. Robert Perske, *New Directions for Parents of Persons Who Are Retarded* (Nashville: Abingdon Press, 1973), p. 8.
3. Peg Rankin, *Yet Will I Trust Him* (Ventura, CA: Regal Books, 1980), p. 136.
4. Jim Conway, "How to Handle Crises." *Today's Christian Woman*, Fall 1980, p. 41.
5. Eugene T. McDonald, *Understand Those Feelings* (Pittsburg: Stanwix House, Inc., 1962), p. 30.
6. Lisa Blumberg, "The Fruits of Guilt." *The Exceptional Parent*, June 1980, p. 21.
7. Perske, *New Directions*, p. 8.
8. Norm Wright, "A New Home for Matthew," *Family Life Today*, June 1980, p. 14.
9. March of Dimes.
10. Steve Zeisler, Peninsula Bible Church, 1980.
11. Philip Yancey, *Where Is God When It Hurts?* (Grand Rapids: Zondervan Publishing House, 1977), pp. 73,74.
12. Ibid, p. 73.
13. Joni Eareckson and Steve Estes, *A Step Further* (Grand Rapids: Zondervan Publishing House, 1978), p. 35.
14. Margaret Johnson, *Beyond Heartache* (Grand Rapids: Zondervan Publishing House, 1979), p. 60.
15. Rankin, *Yet Will I Trust Him*, p. 69.
16. Eareckson and Estes, *A Step Further*, p. 127.

17. Virginia Escher, "Is Suffering Part of God's Plan for His Children?" *Good News Broadcaster*, copyright 1980 by the Good News Broadcasting Association Inc.

18. Edith Schaeffer, *Affliction* (Old Tappan, NJ: Fleming H. Revell, Co., 1978), p. 26.

19. Yancey, *Where Is God When It Hurts?* p. 97.

20. John Gliedman and William Roth, *The Unexpected Minority* (New York: Harcourt, Brace, Jovanovich, 1980), p. 57.

21. Victor Frankl, *Man's Search for Meaning*, rev. ed. (Chicago: Beacon Press, Inc., 1969), p. 104.

22. Linda Tschirhart Sanford, "Make Children Feel Good," *Family Circle*, November 1980, p. 33.

23. George W. Paterson, *Helping Your Handicapped Child* (Minneapolis: Augsburg Publishing House, 1975), p. 33.

24. Bruce Narramore, *You're Someone Special* (Grand Rapids: Zondervan Publishing House, 1978), p. 70.

25. Paterson, *Helping Your Handicapped Child*, p. 60.

26. Gliedman and Roth, *The Unexpected Minority*, p. xiii.

27. Ibid, p. 71.

28. Adapted from Bill Gothard, Institute in Basic Youth Conflicts.

29. Narramore, *You're Someone Special*, p. 11.

30. Public address by C. Everett Koop, reported by Cynthia Scott in *Moody Monthly*, February 1981, p. 20.

Part II

CHALLENGED PARENTING—THE PRACTICALITIES

(Some of the material in chapter 8 is adapted from "My Something Special Children," an article by Bonnie G. Wheeler that appeared in the November 1977 issue of *Moody Monthly*.)

PARENTS' BILL OF RIGHTS

Parents are acutely aware of their responsibilities to provide for their offspring, but are seldom aware of the rights they also have as parents of a child who has a handicap, and as just plain people.

Freedom to:
1. Feel that you have done the best you can
2. Enjoy life as intensely as possible, even though you have a handicapped child
3. Let your handicapped child have his or her own privacy
4. Have hostile thoughts once in a while without feeling guilty
5. Enjoy being alone at times
6. Say at times that you don't want to talk about your problems; say, "I'm tired of talking about my handicapped child"
7. Lie once in a while; say everything is fine; don't feel compelled to tell the truth to everyone who asks
8. Not praise your child gratuitously even though you've been told to offer such praise
9. Tell your child you don't like certain things he does even though he has a handicap
10. Devote as much time as you want to the cause of the handicapped and also to get away for awhile if you want
11. Tell teachers and other professionals what you really feel about the job they are doing and demand they respect your opinions
12. Have your own hobbies and interests
13. Spend a little extra money on yourself even though you feel you can't afford it
14. Have a vacation yearly away from the children; have dates, celebrations, weekends away and time together to enhance your marriage.

Warning: Parents who do not enjoy almost all these freedoms are in trouble. Martyred parents are seldom appreciated by anybody, least of all by their handicapped child.[1]

Chapter 6

THE CHALLENGED MARRIAGE

For from the very first he made man and woman
to be joined together permanently in marriage;
therefore a man is to leave his father and mother,
and he and his wife are united so they are no
longer two, but one, *Mark 10:7,8.*

"The divorce rate among Christian marriages is only a
little lower than for non-Christians."
"Four out of every five marriages containing a handicapped child are failing."[2]

I read those two shattering statistics within the same
week and realized anew what challenges are placed on
any marriage, and I shuddered at the extra challenges
and pressures that face us.

In *Understand Those Feelings* Dr. Eugene McDonald
writes: "While it is undoubtedly true that parents of non-
handicapped children also have disagreements stemming
from problems with their children, the natural emotional-

ity and the complexity of the problems associated with having a handicapped child seem to provide a more fertile ground in which discord can grow."[3]

All the possible strains, challenges and changes that occur with parenting *any* child are present with a challenged child, only multiplied. We have more medical appointments, more physical work, more emotional tensions, more financial strains, more sleepless nights—less time, less energy.

Jane related, "Any child will change a marriage. A handicapped child adds a challenge to your strength, emotions and ability to deal with stress. Our son is a strain on our marriage because I have the principal care and we disagree on his needs and care."

I believe the statistics, I know firsthand the pressures, but I also know parents who believe, like us, that their marriages have been enriched by their challenged children:

"Our handicapped child has affected our marriage in a very positive way."

"Our special child has brought us together."

"We had adjustments and problems, but now we're stronger for them."

And Vicky shares, "Our handicapped child has definitely helped our marriage; through her we both accepted Jesus."

On one side are statistics and wreckage—endangered marriages. On the other side—enriched marriages. What makes the difference?

Building a Strong Marriage

The right foundation. A well-built foundation under a house doesn't prevent flood or fire but it does help our chances of survival in those situations. In the same way a mutual relationship with Jesus—a foundation for a marriage—isn't an absolute guarantee against marital strains and stresses but that mutual relationship does give us an edge against the statistics.

When God watched Adam strolling through the garden He didn't say, "He's lonely. I'll give him a child." Neither did God bend down and make a church or a committee meeting for him to attend, thus ending Adam's loneliness. He didn't even say, "Poor Adam, he's lonely—I'll give him parents."

Adam was blest with the world's first and best pet collection, yet even the entire animal kingdom didn't end Adam's loneliness. With an infinite variety of human relationships to choose from, God created Eve to be Adam's wife, friend, lover and helpmeet. Of the innumerable institutions that now exist God ordained marriage as the first.

In Genesis 2:18 God said, "It isn't good for man to be alone; I will make a companion for him, a helper suited to his needs."

Proper prioritizing. When we follow God's priority system we have a strong foundation for our marriages: a healthy relationship with God results in a healthy marriage relationship. In any marriage it is easy to rearrange priorities and put our children before our mate. Wives seem to have more trouble keeping their priorities straight in this area than husbands (a man's priority problem is usually job oriented). When a child has special challenges and needs we find it even easier to fall into the trap of putting that child first.

The ultimate beneficiaries of this priority system foundation will be our children as we prove the saying, "The most important thing a mother can do for her children is to love their father."

A Wise Investment

When I look back on our twenty-year marriage, and observe the marriages of other challenged parents, one word keeps popping up—WORK! The marriages I see as successful are the ones where both partners are equally committed to making the relationship work.

Some marriages may be "made in heaven" but they are all lived out on earth, and in our case we are surrounded by too many medical bills, too many appointments, too little sleep and too little quality time for each other.

One evening a neighbor dropped in as I was feeding the kids. "Going out tonight?" she asked when she noticed that Dennis and I weren't eating. I explained that I was going to fix our dinner after the children were in bed.

"What a lot of trouble," she commented. "We'll just wait until our kids are grown and then we'll have long talks and quiet dinners."

I quietly replied, "I'm afraid . . ."

"Afraid of what?" she queried.

"Afraid that if I don't invest in our marriage now that when the children are grown and gone we won't have anything to talk about."

That conversation was a few years ago and now the children stay up later than we do. It takes more planning and ingenuity for those dinners but we're still aware of their importance.

It takes extra work to cook two dinners, it takes extra work to make a successful marriage. Thomas Edison once said, "I never did anything worth doing by accident; they came by work." That's just as applicable to a good marriage as it is to inventing the light bulb.

It is essential that we invest time—quality time—in our marriages. When a child—any child—arrives on the scene we can't give up our time together as husband and wife. When that child is challenged and has special needs, time together becomes even more endangered, and this is often a major stress point in a challenged marriage, as several wives shared:

"In the beginning he felt left out; not any longer."

"I spent so much time getting treatment for our daughter that my husband was upset and felt left out."

When we can no longer assume there will be time together we have to plan it. Periodically we go through spells (surgeries, etc.) when much of my time and energy goes into one child. Even though my actual time with Dennis is shortened I'll make a point of putting notes in his lunch, making short phone calls to work—"I love you!" (Once, "I love you," written on a banana.) Dennis might get slightly embarrassed but he does know I care.

Last fall, after Dennis had been through a lengthy illness and before Becky's operation, we made plans to go out for dinner. When we arrived at the restaurant I unlocked the trunk and showed Dennis our suitcase. "You are hereby declared an official kidnap victim," I announced. "You will be my prisoner for the next twenty-four hours. No ransom will be accepted."

"I don't believe this!" Dennis protested. "I can't believe you pulled this off and I didn't suspect a thing." We walked into his favorite restaurant (and later a motel room) with Dennis grinning and still muttering, "I don't believe this . . ."

He did believe he was loved.

It took extra time and work to make all the arrangements (ever try to keep a secret with six kids and when living in a small town?), extra effort, but it was well worth the investment. Just the two of us had a time of uninterrupted conversation, time for a very private communion, time for sharing concerns, time to pray together. The tensions of the past months fell away and our marriage relationship was strengthened and renewed.

On the ride home I kept thinking, *How often we get so caught up in spending our time that we forget it's also for investing.*

Building a quality marriage relationship takes energy. In our lives as challenged parents there will be varying stretches of time when caring for our children is physically exhausting. We need to take the routine precautions of eating right, taking vitamins, getting adequate amounts of rest and being careful to not get rundown or overextended. (I've paid my older children to baby-sit so I could take a much needed nap.)

A challenged child takes energy that would have been spent on other things or other people. We need to review and rearrange our priorities in the light of our present circumstances.

Before the adoptions I was involved in many projects. After the adoptions I tried to keep up with them all plus a rapidly growing family. I assumed that because they were all worthwhile activities that I would have unlimited health and energy. I didn't.

I reached a point where I had to cancel all outside activities. When I was finally able to handle something else I very carefully prayed for God's will and a continued awareness of my limits.

Mutual Support and Appreciation

"Accentuate the positive" was a great old song. It's even better today as advice for a marriage. There is a big cold world out there just waiting to tear us down—unthinking people who stare at our challenged child and ask rude questions, overworked doctors who never have enough time, friends that try, but just don't understand. We need to build each other up—especially in front of our children. As Gloria Hope Hawley writes about challenged parents, "They need to reassure and reassemble each other."[4]

Plan, schedule or steal time to discuss goals and priorities so you're supportive of each other. When Mommy says, "My child needs discipline and order just like any other child," and Daddy says, "Poor baby, can't help himself," there's trouble brewing. As one parent coddles and the other disciplines, "poor baby" plays parent against parent and becomes an unholy terror.

We need to show appreciation to our spouse. "I hope you realize what a sweet spirit your husband has," a friend commented. I already knew that and I continually pray for the Lord to give me a spirit of appreciation.

Challenged parents who reported healthy marriages shared their appreciation:

"My husband is a rock."

"His thoughts and actions are positive."

Appreciation. Building up.

Of course, there were also negative comments:

"My husband used to escape by going fishing."

"My husband wasn't supportive. His philosophy seemed to be 'if I ignore it the problem will go away.' "

"I'm afraid our child is going to think he only has one parent."

James E. Kilgore wrote, "The single most important word in a relationship is *we*."[5]

In society in general there is a growing awareness of the need for both parents to share in the care of their children. Fathers are feeding, bathing and diapering their babies—some even stay home and become "house husbands."

But in many families the wife is still the primary nurturer; and the husband who feels unfamiliar and uncomfortable with baby will eventually feel excluded. When the new baby also has special challenges it is easy for fathers to feel even more intimidated, and mother ends up as the sole caretaker and father as the breadwinner.

That is an unfortunate situation in any family but it is especially disastrous with a challenged child. The challenged mother needs even more help as she tries to cope with more work, more laundry, special diets, and a child that is often less able to help around the house. When mother has the total care and responsibility for a challenged child she will eventually resent both her child and her husband. If the trend continues the father ends up resenting his wife and he blames the child for taking her away.

When one parent is always taking the challenged child to the doctor, putting on uncomfortable braces, always reminding the child of restrictions, it is easy for the child to center its resentments against that parent. And instead of developing acceptance the child develops resentment towards mother—the enforcer, towards father—the evader, and towards the challenge.

Everyone loses.

Almost all of the challenged parents I share with have gone through varying periods of estrangement as the father felt further and further excluded and resentments grew. The strongest marriages develop a strong sense of "we" and the whole family becomes a team.

When life at our house was very tense—two kids in leg braces, one constantly sick, adjusting to life with a *very* hyperactive child—Dennis and I decided we needed some outside involvement in our lives. We signed up for volunteer work at a crisis center (most people thought we *were* one!).

We were in encounter groups, handled hot-line calls, learned to detoxify drug overdoses. Our children were so much younger than the kids at the center that it made for a complete break in our routine.

Dennis and I were each gone one evening a week. One of us was always with the kids at home, and even though we didn't work together in our volunteer group we had a shared outside interest.

It is so easy to get bogged down in our own lives that everything revolves around *our* challenged children, *our* stresses, *our* problems—an unhealthy situation for everyone involved with us.

What are your interests, what would you *really* like to do? Learn to play the piano? Take a night class? Join a bowling team? Examine your schedule and your energy level and talk with your spouse, ask God's guidance and get a new perspective on your life.

Don't Neglect the Obvious

So-called "normal" marriages usually list *sex* and *communication* as areas in a relationship that go sour. Challenged marriages also have problems in these areas—usually more so.

Time, energy, and sex go together like the proverbial horse and carriage. Only in our case, fatigue and time pressure aren't the only elements working against us. For many challenged parents, *fear* is also an unwelcome intruder in the bedroom: fear of another challenged child. The fear often produces frigidity and impotence, and often that fear is needless.

One young mother wrote, "My husband has been impotent since the birth of our handicapped child (now two years old). We haven't sought professional help, we're just trying to work things out on our own . . . and waiting."

That is tragic and probably unnecessary! It is essential for parents of handicapped children to get counseling from a trusted, informed physician: What caused this? Could it have been prevented? Will it happen again? What are the chances of another child being affected?

Many challenging conditions are medical "flukes" caused by accident or illness, and will never happen again. In the smaller percentage, where there is evidence of a genetic problem, counseling with a genetics specialist can help concerned parents make informed decisions about future pregnancies, and eliminate needless fears.

The key is seeking help and information early. It's

much easier to prevent a potential sex problem than to try to undo one that becomes established.

If a mother devotes herself exclusively to caring for her challenged child the father will feel increasingly separated from his wife and child. When there is little or no closeness in the daytime it is difficult to develop closeness in the bedroom.

Fatigue is a problem with many couples. It can be a special problem with challenged parents because our job is so often exhausting.

There are times when I seem to spend more hours with the doctor than my husband; times of sleepless nights and dragging days. And as James Dobson so succinctly says, "Tired bodies make for tired sex."[6]

Once again, we need to realize the importance of our marriage relationship and keep it as a priority second only to our relationship with God. Too often we assume, "He knows I'm tired," and he's really thinking, "Rejected again!" We need to learn to communicate. Betty needs to say, "Dear, I'm not rejecting you, but I haven't slept for two nights, can we make a date for tomorrow night?" Harry needs to understand, "If I help more with little Harry then you'll have more time for me."

Take a nap, go for a walk, get away for a weekend. Save energy for each other. When we make an effort to develop and maintain intimacy in the rest of our marriage relationship it will carry over into the bedroom.

Parents of a challenged child can't neglect their sexual relationship. But close on the heels of sex is *communication*. I have listened to tapes and sermons, worked on Bible studies, attended seminars, sat in on group discussions and always the one recurring key to a good marriage is communication.

Ann Landers, our country's leading authority on just about everything, says that she believes that the most important single ingredient in a marriage is the ability to communicate with each other.

Good communication doesn't guarantee us a problem-free marriage, but like that strong foundation, it certainly does help. Communication includes sharing fears, plans, hopes and dreams. I know my husband's plans and goals for our children and he knows that there are days when I fantasize about life in a retirement community (they don't allow children!).

If communication is the key to marriage then its importance is magnified in a challenged marriage where so much of what we need to communicate is charged with emotion.

A couple going through the mourning process find it is so easy to turn inward. As one mother shared, "It was hard for my husband and me to communicate. We would hold each other for comfort but we couldn't talk about our child. Initially I got more support from my friends because they weren't as directly hurt as we were." But that young couple learned and grew together. "Our child's challenge has affected our marriage in a positive way. Our *need* to communicate has made us closer and able to share our feelings honestly with each other without being judged. Now he can tell when I've had a bad day and will take the kids awhile. If I'm really down he will just hold me."

Another key to good communication was in that mother's quote about "being able to share honestly without being judged." When we're having trouble adjusting to life with a challenged child—the continual medical traumas, financial problems, the stares and glares—we need to be able to share with someone who doesn't judge and make us feel more guilty.

Following are some steps to good communication that we can apply:

1. Commit yourselves to developing communication skills. (An excellent book is H. Norman Wright's *Com-*

munication: Key to Your Marriage, Ventura, CA: Regal Books.)

2. Develop sensitivity to your spouse's feelings.

3. Be patient as your spouse goes through the mourning-adjusting process.

4. Don't be judgmental. Give your spouse freedom to really communicate.

5. Don't place blame on each other.

6. Be supportive. Build up each other, don't tear down.

7. Develop the art of listening.

8. Don't just assume your spouse knows how you feel and what you need. Tell, ask, communicate . . .

9. Pray for and with each other.

Chapter 7

THE CHALLENGED CHILD

God sees not as man sees, for man looks at the outward appearance, but the Lord looks at the heart," *1 Samuel 16:7, NASB.*

I once heard Dr. James Dobson tell a story about his daughter Danae. She was a pretty toddler and people automatically responded to her looks—until she fell and knocked a tooth up into her gum. Her mouth became swollen and distorted and since the damage was all inside her mouth it looked more like a birth defect than a recent injury. Suddenly people were seeing and responding to Danae differently: they looked away, ignored her, were obviously uncomfortable in her presence.

As Dr. Dobson related the story of his daughter's temporary disfigurement I thought of our children with leg braces, hearing aids, wheelchairs, uncontrollable motions and behaviorisms. Danae Dobson did nothing to earn the attentions given her for her beauty; she did nothing to deserve the negative reactions after her injury. Her lip eventually healed and people once again showered her with attention. But challenged children carry their disfigurements permanently.

I rebel strongly at society's emphasis on physical beauty and perfection. Yet another part of me accepts the reality (reluctantly) and wonders, *How can I make my children more acceptable? What practical, positive steps can I take to improve the image my children project to the world?*

Appearances Do Count!

While realizing that society puts too much emphasis on external beauty I also know from personal experience that when I'm speaking before a group I make sure I'm dressed appropriately—my hair is neat and clean, I look as good as I can. Then I can relax and concentrate on the message I'm sharing. But if I'm in formal dress and everyone else is in jeans, or if that was the day my hair died, or if I have a cold sore the size of the Grand Canyon, then I get so concerned about how badly I look that I can't concentrate on the message I have to share.

I'm aware of this, I can reason it all out. But what about Becky? No one else she sees at school wears white high-top shoes, no one else is in heavy leg braces, no one else takes a wheelchair to school. And people react to her equipment and her awkward gait. These are facts of everyday life for her which don't go away like swollen lips and cold sores.

We owe it to our challenged children to help them fit in with other children as much as possible so they will be able to concentrate on more important things.

In our first apartment building there was a little girl with cerebral palsy. Her body was twisted, her eyes badly crossed and she always reeked of urine. I found it almost impossible to react to her in a positive way.

We know a boy with Down's syndrome who had a horrid institutional-looking haircut and a terminally runny nose. His appearance labeled him as different before his behavior did.

I love children. I especially love challenged children. But in spite of that love I reacted to the looks and smells of those children.

When we first saw Melissa she wore bulky body aids. She had on old-fashioned glasses with scratched lens. Her short hair was matted and broken, hacked out around her ears. Two huge hearing aids stuck out of her ears and wires ran down her neck and were attached to square packages of batteries that she wore on an undervest. Over her vest was a tight jersey shirt that outlined the battery packs. People noticed her and reacted—negatively. God enabled us to look beyond the ugly wrappings and see the dainty little girl hidden inside. Most people don't have time.

Improving Appearances

During her preschool years Becky attended a school for the handicapped. The school's letterhead stated, "Behold first the child and then the handicap." Toria was a perfect example of that motto. Her long blonde ponytails were tied with ribbons that matched her dress. Her dress matched her schoolbook bag and her bag matched her wheelchair cover. I always reacted to her cuteness first, then realized and remembered her challenge last.

When Becky got her first wheelchair I borrowed Toria's pattern and made Becky three wheelchair covers with matching book bags to hang in back. I initially made dresses to match each cover but I was careful to get material in basic colors, knowing the covers and bags would outlive the dresses.

And then Melissa arrived! I gave her a careful inventory: her haircut accentuated her hearing aids, making them look huge; the old-fashioned, scratched glasses accentuated her blindness; the unmatched, ill-fitting clothes made her look like an undernourished alien.

With visions of Toria dancing through my head I determined to accentuate Melissa's positives. I washed and conditioned her dry, broken hair; then conditioned it again. I pulled her hair back into ponytails and tied them with ribbons. I got stylish new glasses with clear lenses and bought loose smock tops to fit over her bulky battery packs. Her clothes were color coordinated and the right size. She looked pretty and much more "normal." She still was multiply-challenged, she still had some strange behaviorisms, but people started reacting to her in a much more positive way.

Strangers look at Becky's wheelchair, Melissa's hearing aids and see these as *part of* the girls, not merely something the girls use. But by dressing them nicely (not expensively) I minimize the equipment and give others a chance to really see the girls.

Hair care. The needs for each of our children will vary from challenge to challenge, child to child. Many rubella children have very dry, brittle hair which requires a lot of conditioners. When Melissa wore her hair in ponytails I used only the coated bands that didn't further split her hair. I talked to the audiologist to see if her hair *had* to be cut around her ears, not touching the hearing aids. There were no such restrictions. Melissa is now thirteen and has outgrown the ponytails, but she still takes no part in grooming her own hair. One of the natural look perms was an easy to care for yet fashionable solution.

Becky cares for her own hair and as soon as it gets too long she cries from the tangles. A short Afro looks good on her and is easy to care for.

If you have trouble analyzing your child's hair needs, splurge on a trip to the local beauty shop or barber and enlist their help. Notice the hairstyles of children at your neighborhood school and try to combine practicality with current styles.

Clothes. Clothing for any child needs to be durable and easily cleaned. For kids that are often incontinent or who fall frequently, durable is a necessity and wash and wear a modern miracle. When Julie was younger and in cumbersome leg braces I made smock dresses that didn't bind her metal leather-covered waistband. When she wanted to wear slacks I made ones with loose elastic waists that could fit over her braces. It's been easier to buy ready-made pants for Becky, and I try to keep a supply of cute patches to cover the frequent holes in the knees of her pants.

Having had three children (one boy and two girls) spend years in full-length leg braces, I know the problems of working with the cumbersome braces and helping the children dress like their peers.

I prefer for Becky to wear dresses. I like them on little girls and they're easier for Becky to manage, but—"All the other girls wear pants." I looked and she was right. This year Becky is wearing pants.

When Toria wanted jeans "like everybody else" and her mother couldn't find any that would fit over her braces, she made them. If you can't sew there are usually people in the community who can sew for your child's special needs, or you can trade skills with a sewing friend.

When I shop for Becky and Melissa I look for clothes that are stylish and durable and that they can get off and on by themselves, thus adding to their necessary feelings of independence. I avoid bulky ties or bows that would be uncomfortable for Becky to sit against or dangerous if they came untied.

The first wardrobe I selected for Melissa included long-sleeved sweaters and some really nice socks. Then I discovered that one of her special joys is unraveling clothes, especially sweater cuffs and socks. I quickly realized that short sleeves and cheap socks save on both my nerves and the budget.

Shoes. Children with orthopedic challenges usually have little choice in their footwear, and I'm still trying to come up with a method of coercing the manufacturers to design functional yet stylish shoes. Julie always said that shoes which could be attached to her braces came in two choices: ugly and uglier.

When our youngest son was in braces we could find good looking oxfords; unfortunately the choice narrows for girls. When we do have a choice we get the most stylish shoes we can (this usually means tennies). When we don't have a choice I look for novelty shoe laces, splurge on nice socks and keep the shoes clean and polished.

Cleanliness. Challenged children often are incontinent, spill food more easily, fall down more often. It often seems that with our challenged children cleanliness is next to impossible. I've worked hard to train Becky to keep herself as neat and clean as possible and she has now taken over most of her personal grooming.

For Melissa, and other multiply-challenged children, more of the work falls on the parents. Melissa could care less if she reeks of urine or has food down the front of her dress. But I care. So we work constantly at keeping her passably neat and fresh. Not so much for me, not for Melissa, but for the other people in her world.

Following is an appearance checklist for your challenged child.

1. Analyze your child's appearance wants and special needs from head to toe.

2. Talk with your doctors about any special restrictions if the child uses glasses or hearing aids.

3. Is your child's hair styled like most of his/her peers? Is it easy for you (and eventually your child) to care for?

4. Have you analyzed your child's needs as he/she

has grown older and taller?

5. As much as possible, do you allow your child a choice or say in the clothes he/she wears? Do you help your child fit in with his/her peer group?

6. Have you managed to balance style, comfort, and durability?

7. Does your child's outer appearance accentuate his/her positives in such a way that strangers notice his/her appearance first, challenge last?

Teaching Social Virtues

Most of us will need someone to help us at some point in our lives. Many of our challenged children will need *daily* help from others: someone to read, to sign, to reach things for them, to lift or turn them, to bathe them, to open doors. . . . They learn to expect this help from other people. But how do they respond to it?

Many young children are no longer taught the refinements of good manners. I disagree with this trend in parents of "normal" children. But good manners are essential for children who must be dependent on others.

I don't care how cute or appealing the challenged child is—no one likes to be bossed around; a simple "please" and "thank you" offer encouragement for people to help.

When Becky had her recent operation she was *totally* dependent on other people for a full month. When she would smile and ask, "Benji, would you please get my crayons," Benji would risk his seven-year-old neck to get those crayons. But when Becky was tired and demanding, "Get my crayons!!" Benji used his selective deafness and Becky did without her crayons. No matter how much her family loved her, and no matter how sorry we were about her operation and confinement, we instinctively balked at being ordered around.

I've empathized with her, "I know how very tired you

must get of having to say 'please' and 'thank you' when you would much rather get things for yourself." Then I paraphrased the old "smile and the world smiles with you" adding, "snarl and the world snarls back."

In addition to good manners, challenged children need to learn patience. "Patience is the ability to love slowly." That saying is an often needed reminder at our house that works both ways. Becky and Melissa have to learn that just because they want something "RIGHT NOW!" we are not always ready or able to fetch it or do it.

Patience is especially necessary for Becky because the more she hurries the more she falls.

People often laud me with, "Gee, you must have so much patience." (If this were true my kids wouldn't always snicker when they overhear my patience praised.) My usual reply is, "Definitely not! I just get to use mine a little more."

Often what people mistake for patience on my part is just proper planning. I'm not by nature a patient person, so I've had to learn to schedule my days. When our first two children were in leg braces we discovered that it took extra time to get them dressed and undressed. With Becky and Melissa I've roughly timed how long it takes to do certain chores and I schedule accordingly.

On school mornings I wake Becky and Melissa about a half hour before the other children. When we go out we send Becky to the van before the other children. When I don't *take time to plan our time* we all end up frustrated and in tears.

Showing either girl new tasks takes longer—for Becky to do it physically and for Melissa to grasp it mentally. Therefore it makes more sense for me to plan to teach them a new skill on a relaxed Saturday morning rather than a typical Monday.

Planning also helps build understanding: Becky loves

to help in the kitchen, and if I let her on a day when I can work at a more relaxed pace she understands when, on a busy day, I tell her I don't have time for her to "help."

Forming Good Habits

It's our experience that many challenged children need extra amounts of rest and a fairly structured lifestyle. Until she was eight, Becky got sick every time she stayed up past 9:00 P.M. We quickly learned the importance of a regular bedtime. With bus schedules for the girls and necessary curfews we lead a rather structured existence. But as the children get older the structure changes. We're now often on two (or more) schedules.

Challenged children also need to learn to give and share. "A part of our self-worth comes from the realization that we have something worthwhile to give others. Parents who are aware of this need will stretch their imagination to help their handicapped child find ways to give, to share, and to feel needed by other family members."[7]

Our children have all been given routine chores to do. We're a family and we all pitch in (at least most of the time!). While I realize the importance of this, our children often don't and I end up playing the nag or figuring out ways to entice them to help.

When Becky had her first operation and was casted for six months, her mobility was very limited and there was hardly any housework she could help with (the other children noted this with a strange envy).

Becky got increasingly upset. When I questioned her she explained, "I feel left out—I can't help with anything." (This from a five-year-old!) Becky and I analyzed the situation: What could she do? What mobility does she have?

With both casted legs stretched in front of her she could scoot on her bottom and slowly inch her way across the family room carpet. She could raise her arms and use her hands. There was nothing she could do in the kitchen (except possibly dust the floor); she could put her toys and clothes away—but only in the bottom drawers. After our final assessment we had two jobs for Becky—she could clean the TV screen and wipe off the fireplace hearth and for six months those were Becky's Saturday morning chores.

Becky was thrilled at the chance to be a cooperating member of the family again, and the Lord showed me the importance of our basic need to give and be needed.

Melissa's contribution is putting away her clothes and sometimes the bath and kitchen towels. By a unique combination of touch, smell, and her minute sight she is a fine sorter, albeit a slightly messy put-awayer.

Becky rides a bus to school and her brothers *have to* walk. They often put books in Becky's book bag or Robby will give Becky his coronet or heavy coat. Becky is helping—"I'm needed."

As the girls grow I am continually reevaluating to see what they can do to help. When Becky had her last operation she said in her most serious old lady voice, "Oh, Mother, the saddest part of my operation is not being able to help you set the table."

Teaching Independence

Melissa will always need a protected environment, but Becky and many of our challenged children are capable of living independent lives and independence doesn't just happen overnight.

We need to avoid overprotecting our children. We need to permit and encourage our challenged children to do as much as they possibly can. Overprotection limits experience and prevents the growth of self-confidence.[8]

We need to help our children see each new task or achievement as an advantage, not an obstacle or block. After Becky's last surgery she couldn't lift her ankles (they were very stiff after casting). She started using a walker and did fine on a flat surface, but the thick pile of the bathroom carpet defeated her. She was thrilled at being out of the casts after seven weeks, and her fledgling steps were weeks ahead of schedule, but she started to cry when she couldn't lift her foot up over the rug pile. Her frustration was growing and I said a quick prayer for *great* wisdom.

"Ladies and gentlemen," I announced, "here we have Becky Wheeler, the great mountain climber. Will she make it on this attempt? Or try again tomorrow? OK Becky, careful now—concentrate on this big mountain!" The tears stopped, she got the giggles and struggled to play my silly game and climb the "mountain." Her obstacle became an adventure and her self-image got a needed boost when she finally conquered the mountain.

And the Lord showed me once again that often "great wisdom" comes disguised as plain old common sense or a silly sense of humor.

Many of our challenged children spend much of their time in protected environments. They attend specially designed schools where there is always a teacher or an aide in sight. They are under our constant watch and care at home.

The year Becky was mainstreamed into our neighborhood school I started getting daily reports from her brothers about "the really dumb" things Becky was doing at school. One day she actually ran over a boy with her wheelchair "because the kids told me to!"

Becky is usually a good child, usually a bright child, and we were puzzled by her behavior. I got in touch with some of the other mothers from her old school and discovered that they were having the same sort of problems with their newly mainstreamed children. WHY?

We brainstormed, talked to the principal and to the teachers, and concluded that our children were always near the watching eyes or listening ears of protective adults.

When our other children were out playing, across the street or at a friend's house, our challenged children were usually confined to the house or yard. Benji at three was making value decisions that Becky hadn't made at six: "Do I cross the street for my ball?" "Do I ride my bike to Johnny's?" Even at preschool the other children were making value decisions: "Do I walk straight home or go to Susie's?" Becky and her newly mainstreamed friends were always supervised and were stopped before they did anything dangerous or foolhardy.

When we talked this over I realized that Becky wasn't even choosing her own clothes (she had a raised closet and I automatically selected and got down her clothes).

After we realized what was happening I consciously started to teach Becky to make decisions. I still got down her clothes, but she decided what she wanted me to get. I consulted her more about meal choices. I tried not to hover or interfere when she was playing. I allowed her to make mistakes.

Within a short time she was making wiser decisions at school.

In his book *Hide or Seek*, Dr. Dobson urges "Allow your child to enjoy the freedom and responsibility appropriate for his age."[9] This comes naturally with our other children but involves a little more creativity with our challenged children.

Learning to Communicate

One of our greatest frustrations with Melissa is her inability to communicate, and my heart breaks at all that must be bottled up inside her that she can't express. When the frustrations build up Melissa has a gigantic tantrum to release the tension.

We try to encourage the very vocal Becky to talk over

her reactions. When people stare or make comments, when she's depressed over her slow progress, we encourage her to talk.

In *The Special Child Handbook* the authors write about another little girl. "She had already solved the immediate problem by developing her own way of coping but she still needed to talk about her feelings."[10]

We've always been honest with our children and encourage honesty in the adults they come in contact with. If it's going to hurt we tell them. We owe it to our challenged children to help them face their present—and future—realistically. We need to build trust into our communication.

Scotty is eight years old. He has cerebral palsy and he plays Little League baseball. His mother told me, "Like 75 percent of all eight-year-old boys, Scotty's dream is to be a baseball or football pro. That's such a normal part of being eight that I see no reason at this age to disallow impossible dreams."

When my short son declares his intention—at age six—to be a professional basketball player, it's a harmless dream. When my still short son—at age eighteen—declares his intention to be a professional basketball player I have a responsibility to at least warn him of the unlikelihood of that profession and point out his other assets.

One of the hardest talks I ever had with Becky was over her future. She was seeing challenged children, but no challenged adults, so she reasoned that there was an age when all the problems magically disappear. Her dreams of being a missionary nurse or the first woman president were acceptable (and knowing her, even possible!). However, I worried about her waiting to "outgrow" cerebral palsy. Also, with that attitude, therapy and surgeries lost much of their importance.

Reluctantly I sat down with her and explained,

"Becky, when you grow up, you might be a little stronger and walk a little straighter but you will still have cerebral palsy."

I often feel that life is like a teeter-totter. I have to balance building unrealistic expectations with not breaking my children's will by constantly telling them "You can't!" "You'll never . . ." to the point where they don't! When trying my balancing act I often claim the promise of James 1:5: "If any of you lack wisdom, let him ask of God" (*KJV*).

Following is a behavior checklist for your child.

1. Are you helping your child develop those manners and attitudes that encourage others to give the necessary help? Does your child see you as a model of good manners? Do you remember to say "please" and "thank you"? Do you respect your child's rights and privacy?

2. Are you often a model of impatient frustration to your child?

3. Analyze your schedule with your child's challenge in mind; where will rescheduling and proper planning eliminate impatience?

4. Is there enough structure in your daily schedule to give your child needed security yet not make home resemble a marine boot camp?

5. Analyze your child's abilities and capabilities. Make a list of strengths and challenges. Assign your child a share of appropriate family responsibilities.

6. Are you encouraging your child's independence? Are you involving your child in decision-making? Allowing your child to grow and even make mistakes? Are you overprotective?

7. Do you encourage your child to develop the maximum communication skills possible? Are you a listener not a judge? Do you encourage your child to keep a diary (and respect his/her privacy!). If your child can't write he/she can record a cassette diary.

Chapter 8

THE CHALLENGED FAMILY

You shall rejoice in all the good which the Lord
your God has given you and your household,
Deuteronomy 26:11, NASB.

Marriage and the family are under constant attack
today. The extended family has become a part of history
along with buggy whips and high-button shoes. Full-time
mothers have become an endangered species. Inflation
and "liberation" are sending millions of women from the
"frustration" of home to the "fulfillment" of the work
force. Time pressure has become a national disease. The
typical family unit is under siege.

When you add a challenged child to the family
already under bombardment the results *can* be devastating. Can be, but needn't be.

No one has ever accused me of seeing the world
through rose colored glasses. I know the arrival of a chal-

lenged child can multiply the stresses on a family. Multiply and sometimes devour.

But the challenged families I know are basically strong and healthy. Any successful family doesn't just happen; it takes prayer, planning, and work.

And challenged families ask questions:

"How do we meet the needs of both our challenged child and our other children?"

"How can we include our challenged child in all our family activities?"

"How can we help our other children understand and accept their challenged sibling?"

"Can I keep our other children from resenting all the time I have to spend with our challenged child?"

I think part of the reason for the healthy challenged families I know is that they ask questions, looking for answers. Initially we are all caught up in the trauma of coping, but eventually the survivors start looking for help and solutions.

With our first three children we had no forewarning or preparation for what was going to happen. It was like planning to float across a smooth pond and being struck by a tidal wave. Suddenly we were thrust into the midst of seemingly overwhelming challenges. Sheer survival became our daily goal.

When we entered adoption proceedings the picture changed. We set up ground rules, we discussed our limits, and we developed a whole new perspective because we had a choice. This time when we set out to cross that pond we were equipped with life preservers and the Lord.

The challenged families I have observed eventually reach the perspective we developed during the adoptions. A place of asking questions, looking at solutions, praying not just for survival, but for victory!

Sibling Empathy

One of the first steps towards that victory is developing empathy and understanding between our challenged child and the other children in the family.

In *The Special Child Handbook* the authors emphasize, "It is essential and practical to involve the other children as much as possible without burdening them with your problems."[11]

Timmy was about eight months old when we were given Julie's diagnosis of cerebral palsy. When he could understand, we talked to him and explained Julie's braces, why she couldn't run as fast as he, and what all those extra doctor appointments were for.

Julie was seven, Timmy three, and Robby an infant when Timmy had his near-fatal head injury. Tim came home from the hospital frightened, full of nightmares and *very* hyperactive. We had to sit down and give Julie an explanation of the changes she saw in Timmy.

In turn, their challenges were explained to Robby when he was older, and his need for braces and his constant illnesses were explained to them. (It was a full-time job just keeping everyone informed!)

When Becky joined our family we had many conferences explaining her challenge to the other children. We also tried to anticipate their concerns: "We know there will be days when you get upset and just plain don't like her. That's OK. Just come and talk to us when it happens and don't feel guilty."

When Becky had her first surgery she had full-length casts on for one month, short casts for five more months. In the beginning the boys were very helpful and Becky was either out of it or in a remarkably good mood.

The day came when Becky was frustrated with her helplessness and became justifiably cranky and very bossy. Robby got upset and demanded, "Why does she hafta act like that?"

I explained to Becky that I could understand how she was feeling and complimented her for being so good for so long. "But, Becky," I chided, "Robby isn't your slave and when you're rude and bossy he doesn't have to mind you."

When Becky went down for her nap I had a talk with Robby, "You've been patient and helpful to Becky. I really appreciate your being such a sweet brother, but you really got mad at her today, didn't you?"

Robby spent the next hour confined to Becky's wheelchair. He could use his arms, but couldn't leave the sunken family room.

At first Robby had a great time. He raced across the room. He tried to "pop a wheelie." He twirled around in circles. And he still had fifty-eight minutes more to go. After his hour I asked him how he liked it. "It was fun the first few minutes, but after that it was awwwful!"

"Honey, you were only in it an hour, Becky's been in it for months. Now do you understand why she was so crabby and bossy this morning?"

A small step for Mother, a giant step for sibling empathy and understanding.

There is another side to helping, though. After the casts were removed Becky had to try walking with crutches or a walker. It hurt, it was tiring, but she had to do it. Now when she asked the kids to help or she smiled sweetly and pleaded, "Please, go get my dolly," they had to tell her no. Robby and Benji got confused about how not helping was helping.

When Melissa was about to join our family we tried eating dinner with our eyes closed and cotton in our ears. Needless to say, it was a disaster, but it helped us all understand what it must be like for deaf-blind Melissa.

Developing sibling empathy helps with basic survival and helps build lasting dividends. *We seldom resent what we truly understand.*

Barbara has six children and one of the oldest commented about his brother Danny (who has Down's syndrome), "God sent Danny to us because there are so many of us to love him." And one of my favorite stories of sibling love is about Lisa, who has cerebral palsy. Her four-year-old brother had been praying for six months that his little sister would be able to walk to the Christmas tree. Christmas morning he stood by the tree and urged, "Come on, Lisa, God and I are waiting."

Open Communication

It is essential that siblings of a challenged child be able to ask questions, complain, communicate and clarify their deepest feelings without fear of being judged or punished.

We used to have conferences when Becky was asleep to give the other children the freedom to ask questions and make complaints without Becky getting her feelings hurt. Our job was to be facilitators, not judges.

Kids have fears and questions: Will I get it? (It being whatever their sibling's challenge is.) Will he die from it? Will my kids have it? Why doesn't Susie want to come over and play anymore?

Communication works both ways. We also need to keep the other children as informed as possible. There have been many times when the doctor has given me information ("We're running tests to see if he has sickle-cell anemia.") that I haven't thought to share with the other children. I'll be extra crabby, teary-eyed, and generally a mess, and the poor kids don't even know why. They each go around wondering, "What did *I* do?" A simple explanation could avoid the problem.

Communication is very important when coping with sibling rivalry. Every family with more than one child experiences sibling rivalry. I love that term. It adds a certain dignity to the noisy bedlam of brothers and sisters trying to annihilate one another.

Becky and Benji consider arguing (my term) or debating (their term) as a major recreational activity. One evening, after they had heatedly covered the merits of corn versus beans, Daddy reached his limit. He had the two of them sit at the table and alternate between saying, "I'm sorry" and "I love you." After they had volleyed the sweet words back and forth a few times they were suddenly and loudly arguing about who said "I love you" last. Benji stood up, put his hands on his hips and indignantly exclaimed, "Becky, I wanted so badly to be kind to a handicapped person today and you just wouldn't let me!"

We need to be aware of the potential for harm there is in a challenged family: guilt on the part of the able-bodied child for resenting his/her challenged brother or sister; supersensitivity from the challenged child who wants above all else to be like his/her sibling.

When Trina talked to her hearing-challenged daughter she always looked directly at her so she could read her lips. Trina's young son went through a time of being jealous of this, "You don't look at *me* when you talk!" When Trina started making a point of looking directly at her son while they talked he was satisfied and soon outgrew the need.

Pat's daughter got upset whenever her mentally challenged brother acted up. "We explained his problems and eventually took them both in for counseling."

Karen's son loved to go into his older sister's room and "rearrange" or mess up her things. "We put a lock on her door so he couldn't any more."

And Barbara relates, "In our large family one child is only fourteen months older than our mentally challenged child and she sometimes thinks it's unfair that her brother gets away with things that she can't. As she gets older she understands more."

Equal or Unique?

In *The Special Child Handbook* the authors stress: "There are very few children whose handicap is so severe that they are totally excluded from participating in normal family life. It may take extra time and effort and perhaps a little creativity but there are many ways to help your child with special needs be a functioning member of your family."[12]

Time, effort, and creativity are the keys, whether you include the challenged child in family chores or family outings. In sifting through the parent questionnaires these three keys were evident. The other point that kept reappearing as I collated the responses was that parents had learned—often the hard way—the necessity of treating each child in the family not equally but as unique individuals.

I once heard a story about a family with an uncommonly wise mother. After she died, the adult siblings reminisced. "I was always mother's favorite," recalled the first. "I thought *I* was," said the second. They soon discovered that she had given *each* child the unspoken impression that he was her favorite.

When our family grew so rapidly I was having trouble finding time for *each* child. Finally one day Robby exclaimed, "Oh, Mom! You called me Benji again! I'm Robby!" His exasperated outburst pointed out some real needs in our family. I needed to get glasses or take a memory improvement course (possibly both). Robby is white, homemade and four years older than the black, adopted Benji! We had always understood the importance of family unity but Robby's frustrated outburst demonstrated the importance of each child's uniqueness.

I quickly discovered that time at our house seldom comes in big chunks but that there is much value in the short moments that can fit into different times of the day. I've used Timmy's speech therapy time as "our special time"; we've made games out of the physical therapy Becky has to do at home. When I realized that Melissa and I were spending over an hour a week at the doctor for allergy shots I started taking along her books and we practiced her sign language.

We've also used family parties to build up each child's self-image and uniqueness. We hang a banner, have balloons, and serve a favorite meal. In place of our regular grace we each thank God for something we appreciate about the evening's "star."

During the summer I'll take one child shopping with me each week so that by summer's end everyone has had at least one turn alone with me. Dennis has taken the children out on "dates" for some special alone-time with Daddy. This will range from a movie for Becky to a baseball game with the boys. All positive input and all celebrating each child's uniqueness.[13]

Overprotection of our challenged children can upset family unity and definitely doesn't contribute to *each* child's uniqueness!

There needs to be a balance (back to the teeter-totter again) between the two extremes of having our families revolve around our challenged child and having that challenged child be a bystander to family life.

Barbara says, "Scott has the same amount of chores, discipline and decisions to make as his sister."

Another mother stresses, "I need to be sensitive to the needs of my other children by not shortchanging them while serving the needs of my handicapped child."

And Jane warns, "You need to make time for yourself and other family members."

One of the big stresses on the challenged family is the inordinate number of doctor-school-therapy appointments that are such a necessary part of our lives. At various times each of our children has complained about being left behind. Usually one trip to wait three hours in a doctor's office is enough to convince any one of them of the joys of being left behind.

Barbara's daughter was jealous of the extra time Scott required for therapy, especially when that therapy included horseback riding. The wise mother realized the needs of *both* her children and arranged for riding lessons for her daughter during Scott's therapy time.

Glynice's son developed asthma and eczema during Lisa's intensive therapy program. Glynice and her husband were able to arrange the children's school schedules so they could have time alone with their son. His health problems cleared up and he became one of his sister's strongest advocates.

Family Activities

One of the questions that comes up is about family activities. *Should we plan something together or separate?* At our house planning a family outing is a major exercise in logistics: if our seven-year-old likes it the seventeen-year-old will be bored. If Melissa will enjoy it will we be able to maneuver Becky's wheelchair? By the time I've got it all worked out, I'm too tired to go.

When I asked other challenged families how they handle this, I had an ulterior motive—I wanted some answers for myself.

When Vicky and her husband go on an outing they always take their daughter. "We have no other children and it's probably easier for us. We take Toria everywhere! We went to the Japanese Tea Garden in San Francisco and took Toria—wheelchair and all—across the stepping stones. We take the wheelchair on trails that we've been told weren't even passable by bike. Isolated bystander? Never!!"

Leatha shared, "Our daughter doesn't play well with other children, so some places we don't take her. But we plan special outings for her—the zoo or the park—where she can run and enjoy and not be constantly told no."

Sandy reiterates this commonsense approach, "When something comes up that we can't do with Benji it is kinder to get a sitter than to drag him into a situation he can't handle."

Many other families mentioned treating their children as individuals and planning outings accordingly.

Under the categories of activities and appointments parents stressed the importance of finding a good baby-sitter that the children were comfortable with. Several mentioned that it was such a treat to stay with "Aunt Sue" that their child wasn't even aware of being left behind.

Many adults are afraid of baby-sitting Melissa. "I just wouldn't know what to do." But fifteen-year-old Timmy sees her as his sister and is terrific with her.

Our older children have changed diapers and emptied bed pans. They can cope with a temper tantrum, sign for Melissa, and give basic first aid to Becky.

As each child helps he/she feels part of the "team" and develops empathy for both Mom and their challenged sibling. Our children are asked in advance to baby-sit, they help (that means free) when I have a necessary appointment, but are paid when there are extra appointments or a luncheon date.

Back in the olden days when we only had three children, the Lord brought into our lives a family with a mentally challenged child. Their eldest daughter could handle the child better than either parent and was always missing out on activities with *her* friends to care for the little one. That lesson has never left me.

When we adopted our three challenged children we were aware that this was *our* commitment, not the children's, and we have been cautious not to make them into permanent caretakers for Benji, Becky, and Melissa.

If I ask for a baby-sitter for Friday night and everyone

has plans, I either get an outside baby-sitter or I stay home. Our older children are only *told* to baby-sit during emergency situations.

Admittedly these are challenging times for all families, but as the Lord works in each of our challenged families and we ask for and follow His directing we can truly "rejoice in all the good which the Lord . . . has given [our] households."

Family Checklist

1. Does your family revolve around your challenged child to the neglect of your other children?

2. Are you aware of sibling rivalry? Do you take constructive steps to keep this from becoming a big problem?

3. Do you treat *all* your children as unique individuals?

4. Do you help your children understand each other's challenges?

5. Do you encourage open, honest communication from your other children about their feelings for their challenged sibling?

6. Do you plan a balance of activities that are eventually enjoyable to all?

7. Do you have a balance between having your other children help in the care of your challenged child without overwhelming them with responsibilities?

NOTES PART II

1. Parents' Bill of Rights by Sol Gordon, reprinted by permission from "Survival Guide for People Who Have Handicaps," *The Pipeline*, January/February, 1981.

2. Joni and Friends, *All God's Children* (Woodland Hills, CA: Joni and Friends, 1981).

3. Eugene T. McDonald, *Understand Those Feelings* (Pittsburg: Stanwix House, Inc., 1962), p. 125.

4. Gloria Hope Hawley, *Frankly Feminine* (Cincinnati: Standard Publishing Co., 1981), p. 80.

5. James E. Kilgore, *Try Marriage Before Divorce* (Waco: Word Books, 1978).

6. James C. Dobson, *What Wives Wish Their Husbands Knew About Women* (Wheaton, IL: Tyndale House Publishers, 1975), p. 128.

7. George W. Paterson, *Helping Your Handicapped Child* (Minneapolis: Augsburg Publishing House, 1975), p. 33.

8. Public Affairs Pamphlet

9. James C. Dobson, *Hide or Seek* (Old Tappan, NJ: Fleming H. Revell, 1974).

10. Joan McNamara and Bernard McNamara, *The Special Child Handbook*, (New York: Hawthorn Books, Inc., 1977), p. 99.

11. Ibid, p. 105.

12. Ibid, p. 111.

CHALLENGED PARENTING—
FAMILY AND FRIENDS

(Parts of this chapter are adapted from an article that appeared in the March, 1979, issue of *Moody Monthly* entitled "My Legs Don't Work" by Bonnie G. Wheeler.)

BEATITUDES FOR FRIENDS OF EXCEPTIONAL CHILDREN

Blessed are you who take time to listen to difficult speech, for you help us to be understood if we persevere.

Blessed are you who walk with us in public and ignore the stares of strangers, for in your companionship we find havens of relaxation.

Blessed are you who never bid us to hurry; and more blessed, you who do not snatch tasks from our hands, for often we need time rather than help.

Blessed are you who encourage us to enter new ventures, for we will surprise ourselves and you.

Blessed are you who ask for our help, for our greatest need is to be needed.

Blessed are you who show the graciousness of Christ, for often we need the help we cannot ask for.

Blessed are you who see us as individuals and who encourage our God-given self which no infirmity can confine.

Rejoice and be exceedingly glad, and know that you reassure us, for you deal with us as Christ dealt with all His children.

—Author Unknown

Chapter 9

FOR FAMILY AND FRIENDS

Inasmuch as ye have done it unto one of the least
of these my brethren, ye have done it unto me,
Matthew 25:40, KJV.

As public awareness, legislation, and the visibility of
the physically and mentally challenged increase, your
opportunities for meeting, knowing, and growing to love
a challenged child also increase.

Chances are that a friend, relative, or neighbor of
yours has a challenged child. They would welcome your
help and friendship; you want to help. But . . .

Do you know what to say to a child in a wheelchair?
How to communicate with a child who has a hearing
challenge? Do you look away? Do you stare? Or do nothing at all out of the fear of doing the wrong thing and
offending?

This chapter is addressed to those of you who want to
help us, who want to be our friends, but aren't exactly

sure what to say and do.

May your numbers increase.

Reactions: Mine

"When a person has accepted that disadvantage (of being handicapped) and learned to deal with it, it is devastating to find that the ultimate handicap is not the disability itself but the reaction of confusion, anger, fear, pity or disgust that it often arouses in others."[1]

Every day of my life I cope with wheelchairs, braces, crutches, and hearing aids. I cope with too many appointments and the ever-present specter of more surgery. With all this experience I probably should know how to react to *any* challenged child.

I don't.

Becky and I once attended a birthday party for one of her friends from the School for the Orthopedically Handicapped. One little girl could barely talk and was in a body cast from recent surgery. She looked so forlorn that I ached to say something bright and witty just to see her smile. But I hesitated. I reacted with *confusion*.

Becky, however, went straight to her friend, sat beside her and held her hand. That little girl's smile outshone the birthday candles; Becky's wisdom outshone mine.

There was a little boy at the party who had brittle bones. "Can someone please help me," he politely asked. "I hafta go potty." Several of us stepped forward.

Then he warned, "You hafta be real careful, cause if you pick me up wrong my ribs will break!" Several of us stepped back. We reacted with *fear*. (One brave father did help!)

Several years of challenging experiences have followed that birthday party and one of my peeves has become people who are overprotective and afraid of and for Becky. When she's instructed to "go sit in your wheelchair so you don't get hurt!" I bristle like a momma bear and ache for Becky.

After her last surgery I was having real difficulty dealing with this reaction in *other people*. Then Benji's
spunky little friend developed Legg-Perthes disease (see
Glossary) and had to wear a special brace to relieve the
pressure on his hips.

When I caught Benji and Karl wrestling at the top of
our stairs I controlled my panic and calmly told them to
play someplace else.

Being obedient little boys they went right downstairs—on their bellies! My feelings of panic started to
resurface and after their hasty landing I sent them outside
to play (gotta get them away from those stairs!).

A few minutes later I looked outside and saw Karl
perched at the top of our eight-foot ladder, my panic
definitely resurfaced, and I started to scream—"Get
down before you get hurt!" Just then a quiet voice
seemed to whisper, "*Now* do you understand why other
people react like they do to Becky's exploits?"

It was a much needed lesson in understanding others.

Reactions: Others'

When I enter a crowded reception room with Becky
or Melissa the reaction is predictable. Conversations
cease, activities come to a halt, there is an *audible* silence,
and the stares begin.

Now I don't mean quick, furtive glances. I mean
twenty pairs of eyes glued to a child in a wheelchair, or an
office full of eyes watching a little girl with thick glasses,
hearing aids and strange behaviorisms. Melissa is completely oblivious to the whole thing. Becky isn't. She
once whispered, "Mommy, they act like they've never
seen a wheelchair before."

I had to answer, "Honey, most of them probably
haven't!"

Occasionally one brave child screws up enough courage to ask, "Did ya break your legs?" The mother will be mortified and try to stop her child. But Becky usually flashes a big smile and replies, "No, I have CP and my legs don't work very good!"

Becky's smile and answer often break the ice and the room returns to normal. Other times we sit in strained silence until our name is called and we hear the room hum back into life as we leave.

We all (parents, schools, churches) need to educate nonchallenged children about wheelchairs, hearing aids, crutches, braces, and especially the children who use them. Most challenged children are much better at handling direct questions than they are at coping with the stares of people "too polite" to ask.

Eugene McDonald warns that "parents of handicapped children must expect people's natural curiosity to be aroused by the difference of a handicapped child. Curiosity is not a bad word or undesirable trait."[2]

When we're out in public I find it better to give my children a brief answer (yes, they're curious about other challenges) and then give them a more detailed answer at home.

Jane shared, "I believe my child is here on earth to teach people more about his challenges, and people learn by asking. I tell them to ask my son, if it's a question he can answer."

Mary told me that she encourages people to talk directly to her son, not through him.

And Pat wisely adds, "When people ask me questions as if Mark weren't there I stop and include him."

Leathea said, "Some friends are uncomfortable talking about our child. We're comfortable answering questions and we try to bring up the subject."

Sandy summed it up, "I believe we're to be public relations reps for all challenged children."

I've taught our children simple explanations of their

challenges so they can answer most questions.

Eugene McDonald also says that "feelings of others are often a reflection of your own feelings."[3] As challenged parents we need to be prepared with uncrushable spirits and uncomplicated definitions of our children's challenges as the other mothers suggested. We play the major role in making others feel more at ease and accepting of our children.

I've been amazed at the questions people will ask in front of a challenged child. Questions they would never think of asking in front of a similarly challenged adult.

Becky's first surgery was preventative and the medical prognosis was that she would never walk. This was all explained to Becky. People were constantly asking, "When will you walk?" They were concerned and loving, but Becky didn't need those reminders.

It's been noted that many older people show off surgical scars like trophies and often try to outdo each other in describing all the details. Children don't seem to share this enthusiasm.

Becky has had major orthopedic surgery twice in the past four years and each surgery involved several procedures. We've always given Becky honest explanations at her age level about the coming procedure, but we didn't dwell on it. "*Exactly* what will they do?" is our most frequent pre-op question. I usually leave the answering to Becky. "They're gonna fix my hips and do a bunch of other stuff."

Becky's last surgery was typical of cerebral palsy. She had surgical procedures done for her hips, heel cords, and feet. Pins and wires were put through her ankles to keep them positioned. There were to be seven weeks of casts, five of those weeks flat on her back or tummy. Maintenance. Prevention. And if it didn't work she would be back within the year for bone surgery. We all knew God was more than adequate, we were trusting and we were prepared. We weren't excited!

Loving, sweet people came to see Becky and enthused, "Oh, Becky, when it's all over you'll walk like everybody else."

"Just think—when this is done you'll be able to skate and ride a bike like other kids."

The assumption was that surgery was a cure. For many of our children it isn't. And I was left to wipe up the tears after the "comforters" had gone.

Our friend Sandy came over the night before Becky was to enter the hospital. She and Becky had a private talk. "Bec, do you remember I told you that I had polio when I was a little girl? I had surgery and I was scared . . ." Sandy shared those feelings, showed Becky a few scars, and talked of her recovery. Becky was able to admit she was scared and they prayed together.

Sandy offered no lofty promises, asked no uncomfortable questions. She talked directly to Becky and helped her talk out her fears.

She held Becky tight and they prayed.

People often make assumptions. "If I yell very loud a person with a hearing impairment will hear me." "People in wheelchairs are retarded." Many challenged mothers reported that one of their peeves is people who assume that because a child can't hear or walk that they are also mentally challenged. I've had challenged adults who used wheelchairs tell me of time after time when people have spoken over or around them but never *to* them.

Becky fell once and cut her chin. The emergency room doctor glanced at Becky's wheelchair and asked in slow, measured tones, "Can she understand what I'm saying?"

With tears in her eyes and blood on her chin, Becky piped up, "I understand. It's my chin that hurts and my legs that don't work!"

I've learned that it's always safer to assume that every

child I meet is intelligent and communicative no matter what condition his/her speech or body is in.

If the child is mentally challenged and can't answer he/she won't be offended, and I've avoided the damage that can be done to a bright child's self-image when people make automatic assumptions about his/her intelligence.

Common Courtesies

For some strange reason people tend to forget common courtesy around a wheelchair. We once went to a bookstore to see Joni Eareckson. Becky got Joni's autograph, they compared wheelchairs, and we started to move on. We couldn't! People surrounded us.

Just as I decided we would have to stay until closing time, Joni requested, "Please move so the little girl can get through." No one moved. In desperation I gave my biggest smile and warned, "If you don't move we run over toes!" They moved.

Well-mannered people will rush to open a door for a mother pushing a baby stroller. But a mother struggling with a wheelchair will seldom get help. For six years I've lifted Becky's wheelchair in and out of our van. I've had two offers of help. One from a young boy, one from an elderly man.

Let me assure you, I wasn't offended by either offer.

Over the years I've developed an aversion to giving *unsolicited advice* to others. Most of us challenged parents are the recipients of so much advice that I find myself afraid to dispense it.

Karen shares, "One of my frustrations is the well-intentioned but really heartless sidewalk superintendents who offer all kinds of worthless advice, and who either deny my right to feelings or reinforce my guilt and negative self-image. Even the doctor does it!"

Friend: "Have you tried Vitamin C (A,D,E: whatever

is popular at the time)?"

Friend: "An anti-spasmodic? You mean you're *drugging* that child?"

Friend: "A chiropractor I know treats this with chopped parsley and garlic!"

Neighbor: "A cleaner house might help!"

Karen finished with, "We need our friends, bless 'em, but sometimes we just need them to be quiet!"

A friend of Joni Eareckson lost her three-year-old son to cancer and someone said to the bereaved mother, "I'm praying for you, honey. Praise the Lord." The mother related, "The way she said, 'Praise the Lord,' made me feel like I didn't have any right to cry if I was trusting the Lord. Maybe she didn't know that trusting the Lord doesn't rule out crying. Maybe she forgot that God told us to weep with those who weep."[4]

And in *Yet Will I Trust Him*, author Peg Rankin is talking about illness: "There is tremendous harm being done today in the name of Jesus Christ. The sick are being made to feel guilty."[5]

This is so applicable to challenged parents. More than advice, more than judgments, we need understanding listeners.

Jim Conway has two perspectives on the *art of listening*. He is a pastor who spends much time listening to others. He has also been a hurting parent when his daughter had a leg amputated. In an article Rev. Conway shares, "We try to keep people from spilling their grief because we ourselves can't handle it. We say 'cheer up' or 'look on the bright side.' " He admonishes, "Galatians 6:2 tells us to bear one another's burdens. We can't if we are unwilling to even listen to the burden or bear the grief."

He continues, "People don't have to have answers to minister to me. When you show you care by your willingness to listen that's far more helpful than answers."[6]

We dearly love these children God has entrusted to us, but we need to talk out our fears and frustrations. We need to be listened to, not judged. We need your prayers.

Many people (especially family members) have the notion that discipline and occasional complaints are not permissible from us. The first time I attended a parent's support group at Becky's school we shared how "rotten" our kids had been that week (seems we'd all had a bad week!). One mother was in tears, "It's the first time I've ever been able to say to anyone, 'She was a brat!' and not get yelled at." We didn't offer her advice or condemnation, we just listened.

A friend of mine has recently been doing some painfully honest sharing with me about her emotionally-challenged foster daughter. I've said little, listened much. She recently sent me a copy of an Arabian proverb that defines this kind of friendship: "Friendship is the comfort, the inexpressible comfort, of feeling safe with a person, having neither to weigh thoughts nor measure words, but pouring all right together, certain that a faithful hand will sift them, keep what is worth keeping and with a breath of comfort, blow the rest away."

How You Can Help

One of the most important elements in making a challenged family work is having a network of support people: professionals, friends, and family.

I have a friend whose mother-in-law still hasn't forgiven her for *causing* her only grandchild to be challenged. I know people who have lost friends after the birth of a challenged child. But for every horror story there are dozens and dozens of stories about the marvelous sharing and caring that comes into most of our lives with our challenged children.

Jane related: "Our family and friends accepted our

son as an individual. They don't ignore him, they try to include him, listen when we talk, and baby-sit when we need a break."

Leathea told me, "My mother will take our challenged child overnight and my sister often comes by in the afternoon and picks up the kids and takes them away."

Another mother wrote, "Our family is always there to listen, to comfort, to give us strength from words and touch when we feel like our whole world is crashing in around us."

Vicky shared of practical love, "My sister lost two babies from this disease and my family has been very supportive. My sister and brother-in-law built a ramp off their deck so Toria has more freedom in her electric wheelchair. She feels very welcome there."

Pat is touched when family and friends "show concern about our son's progress."

There are attitudes of love and acceptance that help us. And there are many practical things that can be done to help challenged parents. No matter how inexperienced you are with challenged children there is something here that anyone who is interested can do to help.

Appointments. We have numerous doctor appointments. My record year held thirty doctor-school-therapy appointments *every* month. I had one friend who was honestly afraid to watch Melissa for me, but gladly watched the other children when I had appointments for Melissa. I valued her baby-sitting and her honesty.

Becky attends a huge medical center and I have a friend who goes with us. She drops us off at the door, helps with the wheelchair and doors and parks the car. Inside she helps entertain Becky after I've run out of entertaining ideas.

Melissa is often unpredictable in the car and I have several friends who ride along to help.

Visits. Most challenged mothers are confined to the house more than their peers. Our children require more rest, have less mobility, frequent surgeries, and more illnesses.

After seven winter weeks confined to the house with Becky I cherished a phone call or a friend's visit to share a cup of tea and put me back in touch with the outside world.

Food. One afternoon when I was bone weary from the extra lifting and fetching that goes with a bed-bound child, a friend came by with a steaming pot of soup and hot rolls.

Housework. Glynice told me that because of the extra doctor appointments and intensive therapy which her daughter required she got behind in her housework. "When the women at our church realized how important this was for me they picked one day each week and someone watched the kids, someone else brought dinner and I was free to clean. It was important to me that they met my need where I was."

Time. During one of Becky's convalescences her Sunday School teacher came over each week and read Becky's Sunday School papers to her, leaving me free to rest or read for a brief respite.

Seekers. We have several sensitive friends at church who seek Becky out when she's in her wheelchair rather than wait for her to maneuver her chair to them. If they have time to talk they bend down to Becky's level so she doesn't have to strain her neck always looking up.

Empathy. Our friend was concerned when Becky fell at the front of the church. Becky wasn't hurt but was very embarrassed. The lady she was with reacted instantly and fell to the floor with Becky and they both sat there laughing *together.*

Parties: Many challenged children are more confined to home and are thrilled by "normal" activities that other children take for granted.

One year we invited Becky's challenged friends from school—even one girl in a body cast—and with just a few minor adaptations we played all the regular party favorites.

For Melissa's tenth birthday we invited a little boy from the deaf-blind program. His mother was in tears when they arrived. He was eight years old and it was his first birthday party invitation.

When Becky is invited to birthday parties the mothers usually make sure there's a game or two that she can play and then she's content to watch the ones she can't participate in.

Invite. One of Becky's biggest joys is being asked to spend the night with a friend. A normal activity for most kids and a neat way to give parents and children a needed break from each other. When Robby gets uptight or just wants to get away, he rides his bike for miles out into the country. Julie hops in the car and drives to town, Timmy goes jogging or joins his friends for a rough and tumble game of football. Benji roars over to his friends, or tries to keep up with his big brothers.

Becky and Melissa stay home.

Most everyone I know who works or lives with challenged children could apply Luke 6:38 to their helping: "For if you give, you will get! Your gift will return to you in full and overflowing measure, pressed down, shaken together to make room for more, and running over. Whatever measure you use to give—large or small—will be used to measure what is given back to you."

Friends and Family's Checklist

When you meet a person who has a disability:

Remember that he/she is a *person*—like anyone else.

Relax. If you don't know what to do or say, allow the person who has a disability to help put *you* at ease.

Explore your mutual interests in a friendly way. The person likely has many interests besides those connected with the disability.

Offer assistance if asked or if the need seems obvious, but don't overdo it or insist on it. Respect the person's right to indicate the kind of help needed.

Talk about the disability if it comes up naturally, without prying. Be guided by the wishes of the person with the disability.

Appreciate what the person *can* do. Remember that difficulties the person may be facing may stem more from society's attitudes and barriers than from the disability itself.

Be considerate of the extra time it might take for a person with a disability to get things said or done. Let the person set the pace in walking or talking.

Remember that we all have handicaps; on some of us they show.

Speak directly to a person who has a disability. Don't consider a companion to be a conversational go-between.

Don't move a wheelchair or crutches out of reach of a person who uses them.

Never start to push a wheelchair without first asking the occupant if you may do so.

When pushing a wheelchair up or down steps, ramps, curbs, or other obstructions, ask the person how he or she wants you to proceed.

Don't lean on a person's wheelchair when talking.

Give whole, unhurried attention to the person who has difficulty speaking. Don't talk for the person, but give help when needed. Keep your manner encouraging rather than correcting. When necessary, ask questions that require short answers or a nod or shake of the head.

Speak calmly, slowly, and distinctly to a person who has a hearing problem or other difficulty understanding.

Stand in front of the person and use gestures to aid communication. When full understanding is doubtful, write notes.

When dining with a person who has trouble cutting, offer to help if needed. (It may be easier to ask if the person would prefer to have the food cut in the kitchen.) Explain to a person who has a visual problem where dishes, utensils, and condiments are located on the table.

Be alert to possible existence of architectural barriers in places you may want to enter with a person who has a disability; watch for inadequate lighting which inhibits communication by persons who have hearing problems.[7]

TEN COMMANDMENTS
For our Relationships with Persons with Handicaps

1. I am God, Your Creator. I have brought you out of bondage. Liberation is a sign of the life I give you.
2. Remember the Sabbath Day, to keep it holy; you shall be wholly before Me—the entire congregation, excluding no one because of disability or handicap. I am God, to whom ALL shall have access: You may place no barriers before Me.
3. I name you My children: Therefore, let no one else define My sons and daughters. Call no one "crippled" or "disabled." They are persons: Persons with disabilities—individuals with handicaps.
4. Fear not one another: I know the confusion of your embarrassment—your fears—your anxieties. Your brother's handicap—your sister's disability confronts you: You, too, are vulnerable. You are both in My care. You are one in my sight.
5. Know that I your God have placed good in all of you: you shall not look down upon or patronize the person with a handicap. Recognize that the vast areas of personhood shared in common are far greater than

the few differences that disability creates between those you call handicapped and the rest of you.

6. Your cup runs over with the fulness of life I give you. In your human way you define that abundant life to include education, employment, a place to live, transportation, meaningful activity, cultural expression, and civic responsibility. From these opportunities you may not exclude those you call disabled. Your rights are their rights.

7. I place within you varied gifts, abilities, strengths. Do not forget these same abilities, insights and knowledge are in those you call handicapped, crying out for expression.

8. Be grateful for the inspiring quality of life within persons with handicaps, which in turn engender within all of you perseverance, humor, coping abilities, patience, and creative victory.

9. Recognize in that commonality you all share there is also frustration, anger, anxiety and despair, reminding you all of your common frailty and your common need for salvation, and calling you to mission, to provide succor and justice for all.

10. Give ear to My eternal promise, set forth in Scripture, that underneath are the everlasting arms: Hold fast to My assurance to all humankind that goodness and mercy shall follow you all the days of your life, and you will dwell in My house forever. Amen.[8]

NOTES PART III

1. Barbara Adams, *Like It Is* (New York: Walker and Co., 1979), p. viii. Text copyright © 1979 by Barbara Adams. Used by permission of Walker and Company.
2. Eugene T. McDonald, *Understand Those Feelings* (Pittsburg: Stanwix House, Inc., 1962), p. 60.
3. Ibid, p. 63.
4. Joni Eareckson and Steve Estes, *A Step Further* (Grand Rapids: Zondervan Publishing House, 1977), p. 105.
5. Peg Rankin, *Yet Will I Trust Him* (Ventura, CA: Regal Books, 1980), p. 71.
6. Jim Conway, "Coping with Stress," *Today's Christian Woman*, Fall 1980.
7. Reprinted from "Points to Remember . . . When You Meet a Person Who Has a Disability," published by the National Easter Seal Society, 2023 W. Ogden Avenue, Chicago, IL 60612.
8. Harold Wilke, "Ten Commandments," The Healing Community, 139 Walworth Avenue, White Plains, NY.

Part IV

CHALLENGED PARENTING—THE PROFESSIONALS

A PARENT'S PARAPHRASE OF ROMANS 12

As God's messenger I give each of you who work with God's challenged children a warning: Be honest in your estimate of yourselves, measuring your value by how much faith and ability God has given you.

We are all parts of Christ's body, and it takes every one of us—doctor, parent, teacher—to make it complete, for we each have different work to do. So we belong to each other, and each needs all the others.

God has given each of us the ability to do certain things well. So if God has given you the joyous responsibility of being a parent, then train, guide, and love your child as unto God our heavenly Father.

If God has given you the ability to be a physician, then care for these children with all the love and gentleness of the Great Physician Himself.

If your gift is that of teaching, then teach these little ones as with the mind of Christ.

If God has called you to be a pastor, then minister in love to *all* your flock, including the little lame lambs.

Those who offer therapy to weak or paralyzed little bodies let the very love of Christ flow through your hands.

Love one another with brotherly affection and take delight in honoring each other. Never be lazy in your work but serve the Lord enthusiastically.

When God's children are in need, you be the one to help them out.

When others are happy, be happy with them. If they are sad, share their sorrow. Work happily together. Don't try to act big. And don't think you know it all. Don't quarrel with anyone. Be at peace with everyone, just as much as possible.

Chapter 10

THE MEDICAL MAZE

Jesus answered them, "It is the sick who need a doctor" Luke 5:31, *TLB*.

The professional support system we challenged parents use is phenomenal. One child might easily use a dozen different medical specialists and many educational resource people.

In one year we averaged thirty doctor-school-therapy appointments every month. Glynice assured me this wasn't unusual—in one nine-month period she and her daughter saw a doctor or therapist five days a week.

Mind boggling. Time consuming. Necessary.

We parents become—out of necessity—paramedics, paralegals, tutors, and spiritual guides. This section, chapters 10, 11, 13, contains information gleaned from other parents, physicians, therapists, special education teachers and pastors on working together for our children.

Many of us were raised to believe that doctors and teachers were minor deity with whom we never disagreed or questioned. But we have an awesome responsibility for our challenged children. We don't have the "luxury" of giving that responsibility over to the professionals.

So sometimes we question, sometimes we disagree, but always we recognize each other's value as we work together towards our common goal—realizing the fullest potential of our challenged children.

Doctor a Day

One of our challenged children sees a pediatrician, audiologist, otolaryngologist, cardiologist, pediatric ophthalmologist, orthopedist, neurologist, urologist, dentist, orthodontist, and physical and occupational therapists. She's had five eye surgeries and two major orthopedic surgeries involving ten different procedures.

She's had her chin stitched, her ear stitched and been rushed to the hospital by ambulance (with backboard and necksplint) after a nasty fall with her wheelchair. And she's probably seen fewer doctors and had less hospitalizations then the average challenged child because in spite of her challenges, she's been healthy.

She's only ten years old.

Doctor and therapy appointments are a very real part of our everyday life and it is essential that as parent and child we have a good working relationship with the medical world.

When I took our first child to the doctor for our first visit (at least another lifetime ago!) I was so in awe of him and his credentials that when he instructed, "Feed your baby with two spoonfuls of applesauce," I thought his words were etched in stone.

Then one day my girl friend took her baby to a different doctor. He not only told her to feed her little angel bananas, but he also warned her of the gastronomical dangers of applesauce.

The Bible records Christ's endorsement of doctors in three of the Gospels, and Luke was known as the "beloved physician" (see Col. 4:14). While I truly believe that a conscientious doctor is a special gift from God, I'm also aware that he's not a god but a human being prone to being tired, and not always having all the answers. When we each get rid of our preconceived concepts of each other we can then work together.

Teamwork with Your Doctor

If your child's challenge wasn't diagnosed at birth, you probably started seeing a pediatrician or your family doctor for routine baby care.

One day you noticed that something was wrong: you had a baby who didn't react to loud noises or didn't roll over on schedule. The following *early warning signs* are *some* of the more common indications that a problem *may* exist.

Seeing: If your child . . .
- is often unable to locate and pick up small objects which have been dropped
- frequently rubs eyes or complains that eyes hurt
- has reddened, watering or encrusted eyes
- holds head in a strained or awkward position (tilts head to either side—thrusts head forward or backward) when trying to look at a particular person or object
- sometimes or always crosses one or both eyes.

Talking: If your child . . .
- cannot say "mama" or "da-da" by age one
- cannot say the names of a few toys and people by age two
- cannot repeat common rhymes or TV jingles by age three

- is not talking in short sentences by age four
- is not understood by people outside the family by age five.

Playing: If your child . . .
- does not play games such as peek-a-boo, patty cake, waving bye-bye by age one
- does not imitate parents doing routine household chores by age two to three
- does not enjoy playing alone with toys, pots and pans, sand, etc. by age three
- does not play group games such as hide-and-seek, tag-ball, etc. with other children by age four
- does not share and take turns by age five.

Thinking: If your child . . .
- does not react to his/her name when called by age one
- is unable to identify hair, eyes, ears, nose and mouth by pointing to them by age two
- does not understand simple stories told or read by age three
- does not give reasonable answers to such questions as "What do you do when you are sleepy?" or "What do you do when you are hungry?" by age four
- does not seem to understand the meanings of the words "today," "tomorrow," "yesterday" by age five.

Hearing: If your child . . .
- does not turn to face the source of strange sounds or voices by six months of age
- has frequent earaches or running ears
- talks in a very loud or very soft voice
- does not respond when you call from another room
- turns the same ear toward a sound he/she wishes to hear.

Moving: If your child . . .
- is unable to sit up without support by age one
- cannot walk without help by age two
- does not walk up and down steps by age three
- is unable to balance on one foot for a short time by age four
- cannot throw a ball overhand and catch a large ball bounced to him/her by age five.[2]

If anything on the Easter Seals list applies to your child, or you have other areas of concern, make an appointment with your doctor and start a list of your concerns and observations. The purpose here is not to make your own diagnosis but to try to clarify what the problem may be.[3]

Pat recommends keeping a chart of what is happening, when, and how often. Write down *any* concerns you have. Your doctor can then eliminate those concerns that aren't valid and closely examine the others.

When we first adopted fifteen-month-old Benji, he came with a long list of medical problems and I felt it was important that we get accurate diagnosis and necessary treatment for him. Too much time had already been wasted. Our social worker made an appointment for us at the Child Development Center. It was scheduled three months after we had Benji. During those three months I took Benji to our pediatrician and started my own list of observations to take to the *big* appointment. I wrote down everything I thought could possibly be a potential problem.

On my list I noted his slow response to sounds and his enjoyment of very loud sounds. I also noted the difficulty I had in getting his shoes on. When the child development specialist examined Benji she also studied my list. She thought his hearing was delayed and referred us to an audiologist. When she checked his ankles (because of my note about his shoes) she discovered that one effect of his cerebral palsy was stiffness in his ankles. She gave me exercises to do and advised me on the style of shoes and ways to simplify getting them on.

Even though I wasn't Benji's natural mother I still knew him better, after only a few months, than the doctors who saw him infrequently. I learned a valuable lesson then on teamwork with doctors—they needed my daily observations, I needed their diagnostic skills. We were a team.

Joan and Bernard McNamara verify my lesson. "You, as parents, should be the most important members of the diagnostic team; your feelings and observations should be taken into account in making the final diagnosis. The final decision of what should be done rests with you. This is why it is so important that you speak openly about what you have seen and what you are worried about and that you ask questions."[4]

Evaluating the Diagnosis

As covered in an earlier section, the diagnosis can be made at varying times: before birth, immediately after birth, and anytime during the first few years. Many learning challenges aren't properly diagnosed until the child starts school.

Each specialist uses many different tests to reach his final conclusion. The recording of all the possible tests and testing methods could easily fill another book. For brief definitions of the most common tests please see the glossary.

The Down's Syndrome Congress issued a statement that we all need to keep in mind as we go through the diagnostic process; "It is unfortunate that at birth so many infants with Down's Syndrome [substitute your child's challenge here] are diagnosed as hopeless and helpless. Talk about a self-fulfilling prophecy! Parents are 'set up' with negative expectations for the growth and development of the child."[5]

That statement brought back vivid memories of a little girl I once knew. She was fifteen months old, about three months older than our daughter at the time. Her legs were stiffly locked together and she moved by dragging herself with her arms, army style. Her eyes were crossed and she appeared to be mentally challenged. She hadn't been to a doctor since her original discharge from the hospital.

In her parents' warped priority system she came somewhere after paying for a new car, color TV, and a trip back East. Her parents had diagnosed her on their own—"Helpless and hopeless!" Once they passed judgment on her they didn't talk to her or play with her; she had no toys. When she visited our apartment she was fascinated by our daughter's toys and I was always giving her toys and then replacing them for our daughter. I'm afraid her parents moved to get away from my urging them to get help for her. Their diagnosis had indeed become a self-fulfilling prophecy.

When she was about three I received a phone call from her mother, "We took her to a doctor for her first checkup and he sent us to some specialists. After surgery her eyes will be fine; she has cerebral palsy and the doctors are confident that with surgery, braces and therapy she will be walking by kindergarten."

"And her intelligence?" I asked. I knew it was a rude question, but I had to know.

There was a long pause, finally in a very quiet voice the mother mumbled, "Above average." The next long pause came from me and the mother hastily added, "The doctor says we need to talk and play with her more . . ."

I know that is an extreme case, but it has always been a graphic reminder to me to always separate the child from the diagnosis. As quoted earlier the diagnosis defines the problem not the child. And neither the tests nor the people who interpret them are infallible.

We need to find doctors we trust to get the best possible evaluations and diagnoses for our children. I've always felt that having a diagnosis helped us set up our "game plan." When my neighbor had no diagnosis (other than her own) she had no plan of action and her child suffered needlessly. After a thorough evaluation, plans were made (surgery, bracing, therapy, tutoring) to help that little girl reach her fullest potential. They finally had a positive action plan.

Another danger to beware of when we go through the diagnostic process is how it will affect our relationship with our doctors. "The old adage about the messenger of bad news being the person who loses his head often applies in the case of a diagnosis about a handicapped child. The professional giving the news is often angrily rejected by the parents."[6]

When we find ourselves getting upset with our doctors we need to prayerfully consider the whys of our reactions. Are we reacting to the news he gave us ("Your child will never walk!") or is he truly not the doctor for our child?

There are daily miracles in the diagnostic department. Just this past week I've read two exciting news articles. One told of the successful treatment of a urinary defect in a fetus before birth. The other article was about a new computer hookup that can give fast, accurate diagnosis.

We will often have several different diagnostic examinations for our children. As the neurologist, orthopedist, pediatrician and other specialists each give reports we are able to get a more complete picture of the nature of our child's challenge.

Ask each of the specialists for a copy of his report. Not all will comply, but it's worth asking. Take notes during diagnostic conferences and ask to make arrangements to tape the conferences.

Finding the Right Doctors

Once we've observed our child, taken our concerns to a doctor, and started the diagnostic process, we're plunged into the medical maze. Some of the toughest decisions we will have to make will be in the selection of doctors for our challenged children.

When we moved a few years ago one of my main concerns was having to replace the network of physicians it had taken me years to set up. I didn't relish going through that selection process all over again. The difficulty in selection is compounded by the various characteristics we are looking for in our doctors. Pat looks for a doctor who takes time to listen. Barbara tries to find Christian doctors. Sandy looks for physicians who have positive attitudes, who listen, who don't rush her, and who "answer questions in understandable terms."

Jane reported that "a good doctor will level with you about everything and is someone who enjoys working with handicapped children."

Those are all good, valid standards for selection—but they're all different. One doctor cautioned me, "Many parents look for a supportive, optimistic doctor whether or not he's the most qualified."

I was told to check the potential doctor's qualifications. It's a good point, but what if they're equally qualified? This was the dilemma I found myself in after our adoptions. We were using a medical group that had three equally qualified physicians. They each had equally impressive credentials. I had previous contact with Doctor A and took Becky to him. It was a supreme test because Becky was absolutely terrified of doctors. He was so terrific and patient with her that I didn't hesitate to make him Benji's doctor later. Dr. A encouraged me, patiently answered my questions and always had time to hug the kids.

When the uncommunicative Melissa joined us, I noticed that Dr. A seemed a little uncomfortable with her. One afternoon I had an emergency with Melissa and we had to see Dr. B. He was relaxed with her and they developed a special rapport. I followed my feelings and Dr. B became Melissa's regular doctor. I still thought Dr. A was absolutely super, but they each met different needs. Don't we all?

Most parents suggested asking other parents to recommend a doctor. This works, but isn't always accurate. Once several of us challenged mothers started discussing doctors. One mother described her perfect doctor: kind, tactful, unhurried and gentle.

"He sounds great!" exclaimed Cindy. "My doctor is rough, too blunt and always in a hurry!"

The first mother told us of the near miraculous cures that her doctor had managed. Cindy described some of the inexcusable blunders committed by her doctor.

Finally, one of us asked for the name of that paragon of medical virtues. No sooner was the name disclosed than Cindy exclaimed, "But—but—that's my doctor!" Not two different doctors with the same name, not a case of a split personality, but *one* doctor seen by two very different people with their own unique set of expectations and perceptions.

Someone else recommended that we keep a balance in our minds during our selection process, relying not just on our heads and not just on our feelings.

When I analyzed my selections with that statement I discovered that I tend to pick specialists "with my head." From them I want the very best technical expertise I can get. If I find out that Dr. Barker is the best pediatric ophthalmologist in our area, I will travel fifty miles and sit in the waiting room for hours to see him. I'll put up with his personality quirks and long waits for brief exams because I know that in that short exam he has gathered all the information he needs—I know he's the best.

But for selecting our pediatrician—now I use the "feelings." I still want a qualified doctor, but I want more than just credentials from this one. My child will see her pediatric ophthalmologist once a year. She might see the pediatrician weekly.

The pediatrician will be our main provider, interpreter and communicator. He will probably coordinate our contacts with specialists. He often interprets the reports from the other doctors and, more than the infrequently-seen specialists, he needs to enjoy his relationship with our challenged child.

In my research and experience I've found many excellent points to use during the selection of a doctor, but no one point will always work. (See the selection following.) Maybe Vicky's method is the key, "I pray and pray and pray . . ."

1. Contact your local medical society.

2. Contact the health department.

3. Contact local agencies (i.e. United Cerebral Palsy). These agencies can't recommend a specific doctor but they can give you listings of the specialists you need.

4. Contact other parents of challenged children to get their suggestions and recommendations.

5. Have a brief telephone interview with prospective doctors.

6. Find your doctors during nonemergency times.

7. Question the doctor about his experience with other children who have your child's challenge.

8. Identify what you want from a doctor so you know what you're looking for.

9. If you are dissatisfied with a doctor let him know why; it can help the next patient.

10. Make a point of telling your doctor (verbally or in a note) what you appreciate in him/her. This also helps him

be aware of what is important to challenged parents.

Many of us have negative or hostile attitudes towards doctors. In *Understand Those Feelings* some causes of this hostility are identified:
1. The doctor bears the bad news
2. So much depends on the doctors
3. Our instinctive mistrust of a "foreign" language
4. The waiting time is longer than our time with the doctor.

I'm certain we could each add to the list based on our own experiences and perceptions. Author Eugene McDonald warns about resentment: "Unless its presence is recognized and its causes understood this resentment can develop into feelings of hostility toward professional workers, thus creating a barrier to the child's progress."[7]

We need to make our own list and carefully and prayerfully examine and identify the causes (either real or imagined) for our negative feelings. Our challenged children will have uncountable contacts with the medical profession throughout their lives and we owe it to our children to help them develop positive attitudes. Children pick up on our feelings, no matter how well we think we're hiding them and we need to work at developing and keeping a positive attitude.

Parents' Proper Position in the Team

When we first started stumbling our way through the medical maze I observed all the various doctors treating their "specialty," but no one treated or seemed to care for the whole child. It was as if each had tunnel vision and could see only one thing. Through all those years I was the only one concerned with the complete picture that was our daughter.

At that point of realization it became my responsibility to learn all I could about our daughter's challenge and how it was affecting her emotionally. Often we abdicate our rights to the professionals and don't take our proper position as a team member.

I have no pretensions of being as knowledgeable as the medical professionals who serve my child, but I am the world's foremost authority on my child. As such, I need to assume responsibility for asking questions, researching my child's challenge, and pressing for quality care.

People respect professionalism. When I first started our journey in the medical world I was awestruck and intimidated. I acted like a scared rabbit ready to bolt and run any second. The doctors treated me cautiously, often condescendingly. I discovered that as my knowledge and self-confidence grew, I went to each appointment with more of a "professional" attitude and, consequently, the doctors treated me more respectfully.

One mother was surprised by the reactions she received when she gained more self-confidence, "It was surprising to find that these people were as easily intimidated by my assertive attitude as I had been by theirs."[8]

Sue recommends being calm, inquisitive, and firm. Pat has found that being positive, open, and firm works for her. She asks lots of specific questions and says, "Follow through on a problem until you are satisfied with the answer."

Dr. George Paterson emphasizes our responsibility: "They entrust to him [the doctor] the central responsibility for managing their child's medical care, but they share this responsibility with him in numerous ways: by giving him complete information about their child and background of the handicap; by keeping appointments and following his instructions concerning therapy, medicine, diet, or use of appliances; by calling him whenever they notice any difficulties or irregularities; and by asking questions whenever they are uncertain or do not understand some aspect of the child's handicap or its care."[9]

We need to have enough self-respect to speak up when we don't understand. Sandy urges, "If you don't understand information the doctor gives don't just assume you are 'dumb' and be quiet. Possibly the doctor just didn't explain it clearly and simply enough." If we don't understand we have the responsibility of asking until we do.

Mutual Respect

In *The Unexpected Minority* the authors write about the relationship between parents and professionals: "Both must relate to each other as adults who possess complementary expertise and responsibility for the child."[10]

Sue tells of different reactions from different doctors: "The pediatrician treats me like an expert and the surgeon treats me like someone too ignorant to bother with."

Jane complains, "I get so tired of them acting like I don't know what I'm talking about."

And Leathea shares, "The doctors need to realize that we need support not slaps. Some doctors have treated me like a nuisance, but we are now part of a team and our feelings and viewpoints are listened to and treated importantly. *We respect each other.*"

We need to pray to develop those qualities that will encourage others to respect us. And we need to give the professionals the same respect we expect them to give us.

Professionals need to learn to respect their small patients too. Little Susie is sitting in the examining room happily chatting with her mother. She's stripped down to her underpants and feels embarrassed when the doctor rushes in.

Dr. Smith starts firing questions at Susie's mother and totally ignores Susie. Then he starts pulling, poking, and prodding Susie's spastic limbs. He orders more tests and new braces and hurries on to the next patient.

All Dr. Smith talked about was the cerebral palsy that affects Susie's arms and legs. He talked only to Susie's mother. He treated Susie like an inanimate thing. A few more visits with him and Susie starts feeling less a person and more like a "blob of cerebral palsy."

"Many professionals define the child exclusively in terms of his handicap and teach him to identify his true self with the image contained in the handicapped role,"[11] like little Susie.

When I asked other challenged parents if they had problems with people talking around their child, most not only gave affirmative answers but said that doctors were the worst offenders.

Sue objects to "professionals who seldom recognize the child as an intelligent person first and a challenged person second." Pat adds, "The worst offenders of talking about Mike's problems in front of Mike are the doctors. I ask if Mike can wait somewhere while we talk and encourage the doctors to talk directly to Mike and not through him."

Vicky said, "Doctors think because Toria's legs don't work that her brain doesn't either."

When our eldest son was having the most difficulty with his hyperactivity he developed a poor self-image because "somebody's always tellin' me to slow down or hush up!" To regulate his medication it was essential that I honestly describe his behavior to the doctor. But when Tim sat and listened to my negative recital of his past week it fed into his already negative image. When I realized what was happening I started either calling the doctor beforehand, writing out my observations, or asking to talk with the doctor alone.

Trina has found the key, "I always treat my daughter respectfully and the doctors seem to pick up on my attitude and do the same."

Hindrances to Communication

There are many hindrances to our establishing good communication with the doctors. Often by just recognizing the problem we can alleviate some of the pressure.

It's been our experience that the average waiting time to see a specialist ranges from half an hour to our all-time record wait of three hours. By the time you've tried to entertain any child that long you're both ready for a padded room. And after that harrowing experience you're supposed to communicate!

Let's peek in on a typical visit from a parent's perspective: Sandy Smith and her daughter Nancy sign in, then find two chairs in the waiting room. Sandy looks at her watch and is pleased to note that they're five minutes early. Little Nancy is fresh from her morning bath and excited about wearing her new blue dress.

Nancy gets out her coloring book and crayons and happily entertains herself for fifteen minutes. Sandy uses those few minutes to review her questions and to quickly read over an article she wants to show the doctor.

Sandy looks up and startles three other mothers who are staring at Nancy. Nancy has Down's syndrome. After half an hour Nancy loudly announces, "Hafta go potty!" and her red-faced mother takes her out. Afterwards Sandy reads Nancy a story, then Nancy watches cartoons for a while.

The coloring is done, the storybook read, the cartoons are over, Nancy has eaten the lollipop her mother brought, people are still staring. It's been almost two hours.

Nancy tugs at her mother, "Wanna go! Wanna go!" Sandy explains for the umpteenth time that they have to wait for the doctor. Nancy throws herself on the floor and has a temper tantrum. While her harried mother tries to calm her down, their name is finally called and Sandy half carries, half drags her reluctant daughter to the examining room.

The nurse briskly commands, "Take off everything but her panties, the doctor will be right in."

Half an hour later when the doctor breezes in Nancy is covered with goosebumps and her mother's hostility factor is soaring.

The ten-minute exam the doctor gives Nancy hardly seems a fair exchange of time. "It looks like she'll need that heart surgery sooner than we thought," the doctor says on his way out. "The nurse will make an appointment with the surgeon." Nancy overheard the word *hospital* and starts howling. Her mother understands half of what the doctor says, the rest is in Latin.

Communicate?

Dr. Jones was called out of bed twice last night and then stopped at the hospital to check on those two little patients before he came to the office. He is half an hour behind schedule when he arrives. His first patient is an emergency and the facial laceration has to be stitched carefully so there won't be a scar.

The next parent starts telling him about a new treatment she read about in *Reader's Digest.* "Why don't you try that!" she demands.

The next patient has an ear infection and the little boy's mother is a timid soul who won't ask questions and just keeps nodding yes when Dr. Jones asks if she understands his instructions.

As he rushes to the room where Nancy and her mother wait, he hears a parent talking angrily to the receptionist, "Who does he think he is? My time's important too?"

Then he sees little Nancy. She and her mother are both on the verge of tears and he notices during his exam that Nancy's heart sounds worse. In ten minutes he has given Nancy a thorough exam. On his way out he makes notes on her chart and asks his nurse to call the cardiologist.

Communicate?

From our point of view as parents THE APPOINTMENT often assumes gargantuan importance. It's been scheduled for months, worried and prayed over, and by the time we arrive it seems as though our child's whole future is dependent on that one appointment.

To the harried doctor it was only one of many appointments that day. With such varying perspectives is it any wonder they can't communicate?

Our working relationship with our children's physicians will affect the care they receive and forever flavor the way our children relate and react to the medical world.

Again, the responsibility falls on us—to teach our children respect by example and to develop good communication skills.

Elaine Gollsby emphasizes the importance of family-professional interaction: "I believe strongly that the degree of success of communication between these people is the most critical variable in determining the quality of services provided." Her comments on communication are applicable to all the professionals we come in contact with.

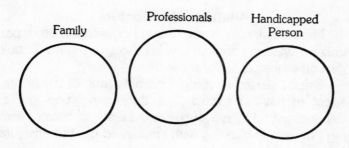

Please note in figure 1 that all participants in this interaction appear equal. Also each participant has both rights and responsibilities, his own part in determining the outcome.

The participants in figure 2 share a common purpose (shaded areas) yet each maintains his own role, his own expectations and his own perception of the interaction (clear areas).

Mrs. Gollsby recommends specific points that facilitate communication:

1. Assume the other person acts in good faith.
2. Permit the other person individuality and some imperfection.
3. Agree upon specific mutual goals.
4. Develop and maintain a feedback system.
5. Finally, work at improving communication skills.[12]

Visits to the Doctors

I had an ulterior motive when I questioned other parents on waiting room survival. I thought maybe I could get some new ideas for myself!

Once I started keeping a running total of the hours I spent in waiting rooms, but the figure soon got so depressing that I gave it up. For the first half hour of waiting I'm usually bursting with creative ideas, but after that it's downhill.

First it's attitude-check time as I tell myself—convincingly—that the doctor is working as fast as he can and that he minds the wait as much as I do.

I mind waiting most when I'm unprepared, so I try to travel prepared for the wait. I put reading books, coloring books, possibly a neat snack, in Becky's wheelchair bag. Melissa has a little canvas tote and we put a couple of sign language books and pencil and paper in it.

I have a notebook that has my daily schedule. I keep a few extra pieces of notepaper, index cards, and a couple sheets of stationery in it. When my child of the day is occupied I can start my grocery list, write my mother, make notes on my current writing project. When Melissa was getting allergy shots twice a week we averaged at least one hour each time and I was able to teach her to sign the numbers from one to ten.

Jane shared these pointers: "We talk, read books, walk around and I teach my child to be responsible for his own behavior." Barb's answer was short, "Patience!" and Sandy wrote, "I have no hints, but if you get any answers let me know."

Sue uses the waiting time to go over questions and calm herself down. "And in the examining room we talk about what the doctor will do. I let my child look around and familiarize himself with the room—but not search and destroy!"

And a few more pointers gleaned from the experts:

1. Be as close to appointment time as possible to cut waiting time.

2. Don't overload yourself with diaper bags, etc.; keep your hands free for your child.

3. Try to choose a day when going to the doctor is the main activity of the day (not squeezed into a hectic schedule).

4. Bring along favorite activities.

5. Stay calm.

6. Keep a sense of humor.
7. Pray!!

When our first child was born I routinely took her in for checkups and shots. Dennis was usually aware of an appointment but tended to view a three-ounce weight gain or a change in formula as my domain. Decisions then were uncomplicated and I could make the momentous decision of whether to start feeding our child pears or applesauce.

When the doctor diagnosed our daughter as having cerebral palsy the game changed. Appointments multiplied; life-affecting decisions were being made. In my uncertainty I instinctively knew they would have to be joint decisions and that *ideally* we should both attend all of our daughter's appointments.

As the years passed and our challenges increased the "ideal" was always recognized, but not always possible. Unless the multiple appointments that are part of our territory are handled correctly they can become a devisive wedge in the marriage relationship and consequently have a devastating effect on our children.

Many wives shared that their husbands felt left out as mother and child commuted to the numerous appointments.

The more the father is involved in the total care (home, school, medical) of the challenged child the less he will feel like a bystander and the more he will be able to adjust and accept the reality of the child's challenge. "A father who is able to go with his handicapped child to some of the specialists is better able to understand not only the diagnosis but also the feelings of his wife and child."[13]

Mary shares the ideal: "My husband and I always attend meetings together where Michael's diagnosis is discussed. We work together as a team sharing experiences, information and the emotional highs and lows."

Over our nineteen years of challenged parenting Dennis has attended as many meetings as he could without jeopardizing his job. But for the majority of appointments I go with our child. Dennis and I sit down the night before and go over points that need to be covered during the appointment, any questions or concerns that we both have, any recent observations we both have made. I write down questions and comments and we review our list.

The next day I go over our list with the doctor or teacher and write down answers, observations, or concerns that come up. If any important decisions need to be made I say, "I'll have to discuss this with my husband and I'll call you tomorrow with *our* decision."

That evening I give Dennis an "instant replay" of all that was said and we make any necessary decisions *together*.

Many mothers mentioned taking a friend or relative along with them on appointments. The two of them can go over notes together and make sure nothing is forgotten and the friend can care for the child while the mother talks with the doctor.

When Glynice's daughter was examined and diagnosed at a large medical center they saw fifty-two doctors in five days and her mother took shorthand notes of all the conferences for their home file.

In spite of our involvement we are discouraged and/or forbidden from seeing our child's medical records. They're for the other professionals. One mother told me she has a complete home copy of her daughter's medical records, but that's not always an option for most of us.

When we lived in one community for many years and our pediatrician had all of our records I didn't realize the importance of keeping home records. Then we started the adoptions and the kids' records were scattered among many doctors. When we moved and needed a doctor before any of our records were transferred I became a believer in home records.

After our move the new doctors wanted x-rays of Becky. That doctor left and the next doctor wanted a different set of x-rays. I felt more in control when I started keeping a written record of Becky's x-rays.

I have a file folder for each member of our family in which I keep medical and school records. I don't have time to keep complicated records and I recommend that you set up and use a system you feel comfortable with. Figure 3 is a sample Home Medical Record for you to consider.

Medication

Our challenged children often require more medications than our other children—from seizure control to antibiotics. The possible interactions between one drug and another and between drugs and foods are almost limitless and it would be impossible to keep abreast of every possible potential problem.

When two of our children were using Ritalin to control their hyperactivity I read every available piece of information I could find. I quickly discovered that each expert had his own pet theory, and I prayed for discernment to read with a balance.

I try to read up on every medication that any of us routinely take and have found that both the doctor and the druggist are good sources of information, but I usually have to ask.

We need to keep a record of routine medications and remind the doctors of medications our child is already taking whenever he issues a new prescription. Two of our children are allergic to penicillin and I'm amazed at the times I've had to remind our doctors.

Becky can tell me whenever she has any unusual symptoms or exaggerated reactions, whereas I have to be very vigilant with Melissa's medication. She gives no feedback and has had two life-threatening systemic reactions.

The most common side effects to medication are drowsiness, dry mouth, and blurred vision.

There are also unpredictable reactions that are often not related to dosage or length of time the child has been taking the medication. (Melissa was ten years old and had used penicillin many times before she had her first reaction.)

The most dangerous or important side effects to watch for are:

- Persistent or severe sore throats; easy bruising; fever
- Abnormal movements of face, tongue, eyes, hands, etc.; increased restlessness
- Skin rash; asthma
- Inability to pass urine or to have bowel movements
- Jaundice (yellowish color of skin and whites of eyes)
- Increase in seizures, or seizures when there were previously none.

"These need to be evaluated in relation to previous symptoms, not just by themselves—they are therefore most significant when occurring for the first time."[14]

Hospitalization

The typical challenged child will have many hospital stays in his/her lifetime. Corrective and preventative surgeries can be scheduled, planned and prepared for. Emergency care from accidents or their more frequent illnesses leave us with little or no preparation time.

When our young son fell and suffered a brain concussion and blood clot there was no prep time. He was unconscious when he entered the hospital and when he regained consciousness he found himself on another "planet." The adult alien inhabitants spoke another language; their native costume was white; and the equipment they used (blood pressure cuffs, IV's, etc.) was foreign to him. The small aliens had shaved and/or bandaged heads, swollen features and were all dressed alike.

Six month later, Tim was still recovering from the "culture shock" of his hospitalization and was still having nightmares of a return trip.

I feel an obligation to my children to do good PR work for the hospital, and I shudder when I hear people use hospitals as a threat. We need to familiarize our children with the hospital. Read them books, let them talk to others, arrange for them to visit people in the hospital. Some hospitals offer pre-admission tours for children.

When surgery is necessary we need to ask questions:
- Why is this surgery necessary?
- What is the procedure?
- What are the benefits for my child?
- What are the risks?
- How long will the recovery period be?
- How much will it cost? Will our insurance cover it?
- What happens if we don't have the operation?
- Are there any less radical ways of treatment?
- Can we have a second opinion (in non-life-threatening situations).[15]

Once surgery or a hospital stay is scheduled we need to prepare our children. I remember overhearing a mother "prepare" her daughter for orthopedic surgery: "You'll love the hospital. You get to watch TV and eat all the ice cream you want."

Can you imagine that child's feeling of betrayal when she discovered there was more to the hospital than TV and ice cream?

Fear of the unknown is especially frightening to children. We need to help them take out their fears and help them identify and examine them.

When Becky had her first orthopedic surgery she was five. I remembered the lasting traumas from Tim's hospital stay and I was determined to help Becky not go through that. Her therapist explained the surgical details and the reasons for the surgery to Becky in language she could understand. One of the girls in Becky's class returned to school from similar surgery the week before Becky's surgery and their teacher made a point of getting them together to talk. Whenever Becky appeared extra quiet or pensive I asked her what was wrong and gave her many opportunities to ask questions.

Seeing her friend return and describe her hospital experience probably helped Becky more than anything we adults did.

Children's sense of time isn't as developed as ours and we need to prepare them for the length of their hospital stay. Becky's surgeon said she would be hospitalized for five to seven days. We planned on the seven. I bought a Bible storybook and taped a lollipop for each day of her stay to the pages. "When you eat the last lollipop you'll come home." That was a time concept she could understand and keep track of.

I purchased reading and coloring books at the Bible bookstore so Becky would feel surrounded by Jesus' love even when she was playing.

We had the elders of our church lay hands on Becky and pray for her courage, our strength, and the surgeon's skill.

The fear of separation is strong in children. When Becky was tucked in bed in a pretty new nightgown, holding her favorite dolly and watching cartoons we said, "Becky, we are going for a cup of coffee and we'll be back in a few minutes." Before we left for the night we had taken numerous trips and when we finally said, "We're going home now and we'll be back at 7:00 in the morning," she believed us. Last winter when she was going back for more surgery we asked what she remembered from her earlier surgery. She crunched up her face in deep thought and finally said, "I remember all those cups of coffee you and Daddy drank that first night!"

I recently ran across *My Hospital Book*, a delightful way for a child to record his/her hospital stay. It's a fun way to keep your child occupied and provide a permanent record of his/her stay.[16]

Most hospitals will let a parent stay in the hospital with their child the night before and the night of surgery. If this can be worked out it can help lessen the chances of a lasting trauma.

When we go back to the hospital as outpatients Becky always comments on two things: (1)"the lousy food and (2) my special *friends*."

Cooperating with Therapy

Our challenged children often need various therapies to help them reach their fullest potentials: speech therapy to help them talk, physical therapy to help them walk and use their major muscles, occupational therapy to help with daily skills. One of our children even had therapy for a tongue thrust problem. When therapy is handled by a professional in a professional setting our main job is to help our child develop a cooperative spirit.

Over the years I've depended on our therapists. They help me identify and clarify my concerns and observations before we see the doctor. During the actual appointment they explain my concerns and observations (along with theirs) to the doctor in the technical language he can understand. After the appointment they explain to me the doctor's concerns and observations in layman's language that I can understand.

When I interviewed therapists for this book my main concern was how we parents can cooperate better in our home therapy programs. I've had to work with two sons on their speech, with one child's thrusting tongue, and with assorted sets of uncooperative legs. I've discovered that once we move out of the professional environment to our family room we have a whole new set of complications. It's one thing for a child to be in a clinical setting with a uniformed person making him/her do uncomfortable things. But when it's "just Mom" at home. . . . After a time of putting up with my unwilling child I start feeling like an army drill sergeant, not a loving mother. I've already had to remind Becky to straighten her posture, not to sit "that way," to put her arms down, put her braces on, and use her crutches. Add a home therapy program to that and it's almost more than our relationship can handle.

One therapist recognized that while the average parent *wants* to cooperate, each one comes with his/her own set of past experiences which affect his/her ability to cooperate:

1. The parents' acceptance of the child's disability
2. Previous experiences with dealing with their child
3. Family acceptance of the program
4. Ability to comprehend and remember
5. The parents' physical stamina
6. Family schedule and responsibilities
7. Other social and economic problems.

When Tim was having speech therapy, and I had to work with him at home, that became *our time*—a special treat for one of six children.

When Becky was younger she could work better with her father than with me. He has a special knack for turning work into fun. As Becky gets older her therapists try to set up a home program that she can do on her own and my job now is to monitor.

It's mid-afternoon as I write this. I spent two hours this morning getting blood tests for Melissa and taking her for her allergy shots. In an hour I have to go back to the neighboring town with Becky for her therapy. I'm still in the medical maze.

Still spending too much time waiting, still working on building communications skills. Nineteen years ago I felt like Alice in Wonderland tumbling into an unknown land. Scared of the professionals, intimidated by their expertise. I've watched other parents try to angrily bulldoze their way through the maze and they're as ineffective in their anger as I was in my timidity.

After nineteen years of daily trips through the maze I'm a seasoned traveler. I don't have all the answers, I still get lost, but my perspective has changed. I know that *this* appointment won't begin or end our life, I know our doctors are human. I still respect them. I know they care.

I know I'm an imperfect human, but I respect my knowledge of my child. And I know I don't travel through the medical maze alone. I'm part of a team and we all journey together towards a common goal—a better future for the children.

Heaven's Very Special Child

A meeting was held quite far from earth,
"It's time again for another birth"
Said the Angels to the Lord above.
"This Special Child will need much love.

His progress may be very slow,
Accomplishments he may not show.
And he'll require extra care
From the folks he meets down there.

He may not run or laugh or play;
His thoughts may seem quite far away.
In many ways he won't adapt
And he'll be known as handicapped.

So let's be careful where he's sent.
We want his life to be content.

Please Lord find the parents who
Will do a special job for You.

They will not realize right away
The leading role they're asked to play.
But with this child sent from above
Comes stronger faith and richer love.

And soon they'll know the privilege given
In caring for their gift from Heaven.
Their precious charge so meek and mild
Is Heaven's Very Special Child."*

* This is part of "This Is Our Life," by John and Edna
Massimilla, P.O. Box 21, Hartboro, PA 19040. Copyright
1956. Printed with permission.

HOME MEDICAL RECORD

Name:
Birthdate
Diagnosis:
Birth weight:
Gestation:
Blood type:
Birthplace:

Immunization Record:
date   shot   booster

X-rays:
date   area   hospital   doctor

Tests:
date   test   doctor   results

Prescriptions:
date   drug   reaction

Severe illnesses:
date   duration   treatment

Surgeries:
date   procedure   hospital

List of Doctors:
name   specialty   address

Figure 3

Chapter 11

THE EDUCATION ENIGMA[17]

But the goal of our instruction is love, *1 Timothy 1:5, NASB.*

Two armies are gearing up for battle. Each has attended countless strategy meetings. Each speaks a different language. Each has a battle plan. Each has chosen weapons.

War is declared!

And on the sidelines wait the innocent victims of all grown-up wars—the children.

This imagery grieves me, but it is one that has kept reappearing as I've worked on this chapter trying to sort through the bias to find the facts. I've heard educators describe the average parent as greedy and grasping. I've read articles where we were portrayed as mentally deficient preschoolers—

Working with Educators

Then I've sat through discussions with parents as they depict educators as Count Dracula, the boogeyman, and Lucifer—THE ENEMY.

My prayer is that we will be able to stop seeing each other as *THE ENEMY* and be able to work together for our challenged children. And so, I dedicate this chapter *to peace.*

Susie has a slight speech challenge and has therapy at her neighborhood school. Stevie has spina bifida (see glossary) and spends half a day at a school for the orthopedically challenged and half at his neighborhood school. Melissa has vision and hearing challenges and is in a special program thirty miles from home. Danny has Down's syndrome and attends a regular class with an aide.

These are only a few of the challenges covered by our nation's sixteen thousand school districts. It has been estimated that some 10 percent of the students in our schools can't learn in the average classroom setting. Eight million American children need some sort of special help.

Until recent years those special needs were met haphazardly, if at all. Many children were improperly placed, many others not placed at all.

Our first child was always part of the neighborhood school and we managed to muddle through the complications of leg braces and mild hyperactivity. Our next child was *very* hyperactive and seemed to have constant trouble at school, but as long as he was *coping* (with a combination of tears, frustration and medication) there was no help for him.

Our "educational" education picked up with Becky's arrival. We learned new terminology and experienced a school program that encouraged parental participation.

Our first brush with special education was both positive and the proverbial calm before the storm.

When the multi-challenged Melissa arrived our education really began. After she had been with us a year she outgrew her school program and was accepted into another. Then she was moved into an inappropriate class. I spent forty hours in that month attending meetings, gathering information and studying the law. We went through due process, an eighteen-hour hearing, wrote hundreds of letters, and felt like Alice in Wonderland, or Don Quixote vainly tilting at windmills.

We were vilified, subtly threatened, and canonized, but we learned! We have met helpful people who donated hours and hours to help us, people who put their jobs on the line for a special little girl. We have met educators who encouraged us and one who ordered (like Alice's mad queen), "I don't care what it takes or costs but get rid of that parent!"

We were rewarded with a new law that guaranteed our child protection but didn't have the clout to deliver as promised. We have seen and experienced the multifaceted educational enigma. Our experience was rougher because we didn't start learning at the first steps, but waited until we were under fire.

How to Proceed

When you first learn of your child's challenge (or suspect it) and receive a diagnosis, you need to take the first steps toward your child's future education. Numerous parents have told me how they regret lost years and wonder, "What if . . ." treatment and education had started earlier.

The law concerning the age at which children start special education programs varies from state to state (many areas even cover infant programs), so the earlier contact is made with the proper program the better. A short phone call to a neighborhood school should get you guidance for the first steps. Explain the situation, ask who to contact for further information, and what steps to take next.

At these first steps we need to remember that some challenges which prevent our children from learning don't show. In addition to the warning signs we listed in chapter 10, be on the lookout for these invisible warning signs and seek prompt help. *Is my child*: overly shy or aggressive? Excessively awkward or clumsy? Easily confused? Easily frustrated? Forever forgetting? Unable to concentrate? Inattentive?

Then make a phone call to the local school (or district office) for basic information and the name of the proper contact person. Record the age at which a program will be available for your child and follow up your phone call with a written request for an assessment.

Even when *you* request the assessment the school district must send you a written notice asking permission to test your child. Legally they *must* have your written consent before any evaluations or assessments can be done.

The next step will be an informal screening. Depending on the results of the screening, an assessment may be done to determine what special needs your child has.

The assessment (or reason for refusal) must be completed within thirty-five school days of the date of your written consent for assessment. These services are provided only upon your written approval, at no cost to you, and with the assurance of full confidentiality and due process procedures.[18]

If the school turns down your request for an assessment they must give you a written explanation of their reasons. If you still believe your child needs an assessment there is an appeals procedure.

The assessment plan must be well rounded and done

by a team of specialists who are familiar with your child's specific challenge. The tests must be selected to evaluate *your* child, taking the specific nature of his/her challenge into consideration.[19] The assessment will cover the child's intellectual, physical and emotional development. It may include talking to people who know your child (including doctors and other professionals), meeting with parents, personal observation, giving tests and (if already in school) conferring with classroom teachers.

Melissa had a full-scale assessment ordered by the fair-hearing panel. It was headed by a child psychologist who had worked with deaf-blind children. The psychologist talked with me, observed Melissa in school, and talked with her prior and current teachers. She read reports from Melissa's doctors and administered tests that were evolved for children with Melissa's particular challenges.

Melissa's assessment included physical and occupational therapy, a speech pathologist, audiologist, and a mobility specialist. Part of the reasoning behind this multidisciplinary approach is that the law prohibits any one test or procedure from being the sole means of making a decision about an education program.[20]

It is essential to share your potential observations with members of the assessment team. In Melissa's case one new teacher described her as a "basket case" to the team. A former teacher raved about her potential. I told about her home life and made my observations. My input spurred the team to test Melissa in areas they wouldn't have considered if they had talked only to the negative teacher.

All the methods used in the assessment must be racially and culturally nondiscriminatory and in the child's native language (everything was signed for Melissa).

Always keep in mind that part of the purpose of an assessment is to determine the child's strengths, assets, current performance levels, and educational needs. Not just their weaknesses.

After Assessment

Once again we must assume responsibility. "As the monitor of your child's progress it is important to have full knowledge and understanding of the diagnostic assessments. Know what recommendations are made and why. Do not hesitate to ask that the test results be interpreted to you in clear, simple terms."[21]

As with the medical diagnosis, we need to remember that the diagnostic assessments and reports are important, but they are not infallible. Occasionally we will need to remind people that there is a child involved, not just scores on a test. Pat has written a big "I CAN" across her son's folder to remind herself of his abilities.

After the assessment is complete make certain that all information used to evaluate your child is documented with the name of the person who provided it.

If you disagree with the results of the assessment you can obtain an independent evaluation. When the school refuses to give your child the needed special education based on their assessment, it might be essential to get an outside evaluation done. However, unless you can prove that the school's assessment was inadequate you had better be prepared to pay for private testing.

It's important to pray for discernment here (as when seeking a medical diagnosis). Stand up for what your child *really* needs but don't just keep searching for someone to agree with you.

What do we expect the schools to do for our challenged children? Teach, train, guide? Or cure and heal? Several teachers I interviewed commented on our expectations:

"The most common problem from my teacher's perspective is parents not knowing what the program actually does."

"Parents want us to cure their child."

"Parents need to understand the limitations of any system."

Ethel Herr sums up what we can expect the schools to do for our challenged children:

1. Help us identify learning difficulties
2. Help us plan a course of action to deal with our child's identified handicap
3. Help us place our child in the best learning situation for him.[22]

Special education is defined by law as "specifically designed instruction, at no cost to parents or guardians, to meet the unique needs of a handicapped child."[23]

Special education includes related services: transportation, speech therapy, psychological services, physical and occupational therapy, recreation, counseling service, medical services for diagnosis, and evaluation.

Informing parents about child development and helping parents to understand the special needs of their child can also be included.

Special education is not necessary for all challenged children since many are able to—and should—attend school without any change in their program.

Our first three children were totally in the regular school system, and we really didn't know what to expect with Becky. She was evaluated and it was decided that she could benefit by attending preschool at a school for the orthopedically challenged. A bus with a wheelchair lift transported her every day. Her teachers were "specialists" and could spot potential learning problems and offer possible solutions. She received physical and occupational therapy at the facility and had adaptive physical education. If she had needed the services of a speech therapist or psychologist, one would have been available. She was part of the special education program.

When the decision was eventually made for Becky to

attend our neighborhood school she was still considered part of the special education program. She had an IEP (see glossary), rode the bus, and had therapy as an outpatient at her former school.

In our present school district she is totally mainstreamed and is not considered part of the special education program even though she still requires transportation.

The educational needs of our challenged children are now guaranteed under *Public Law #94-142*. "In 1974 when PL 94-142 was drafted Congress found that only half of the estimated number of handicapped children were receiving appropriate educational services and one million youngsters had been excluded entirely from the public school system."[24]

PL 94-142 has been hailed as the "Bill of Rights for the Handicapped" and called the "Magna Carta for parent power." I've heard it called much less complimentary terms by the people who administrate it.

Basically this law guarantees a free and *appropriate* (key word) education to *all* children through identification, least restrictive environments, individual education plans, and due process.

The outcome of PL 94-142 depends on how we utilize and react to it. We each have to help make the law work for our own and other children. We have to be cautious that this long overdue legislation doesn't die by default—laws don't enforce themselves.[25]

Some of the complaints against PL 94-142 are: It threatens the educational economic system because of serious underfunding; it promises parents things the system isn't ready to give; there's a lack of local funds that affects compliance; there's too much paperwork for the educators; enforcement procedures are noneffective.

We've discovered the validity of most of the complaints, but it is still a much, much needed piece of legislation. It needs to be revised, not thrown out. *Closer Look* urges, "It will take knowledgeable parents actively pursuing implementation of the laws and regulations, including vigorous monitoring of the procedures followed and the programs offered by the state and local educational agencies."[26]

One teacher told me that "the new procedures give parents more knowledge and make us more accountable. It is more work, but I think it will make us better teachers and pay off for the kids."

An administrator expressed outrage that the state and federal governments have mandated expensive programs and then failed to fund them.

The educators and politicians need to realize that the law needs revision, not recall. And we parents need to remember that even with the law we can't expect the schools to do it all.

Following are suggestions to help us keep this essential law alive:

1. Know the law (learn through parent groups, workshops, and parent training sessions).
2. Work with other parents (strength in numbers).
3. Work with professionals.
4. Use your right to speak.
5. Stop pleading. Education is a right!
6. Learn how to take part in planning conferences—it takes a mix—no one knows it all and your input is important.
7. Remember, don't compromise—insist on full evaluation and clear goals.
8. Be an active citizen.[27]

The heart of PL 94-142 is the Individualized Education Plan (IEP) and the law requires that one be written for each child entering and receiving special education.

The IEP should include the child's current performance level, annual and short-term goals and objectives, services to be provided and who will work with the child. It must also include dates and time lines for specific activities, how much the child will participate in regular classes or extracurricular activities, and an evaluation plan.

Goals written into the IEP are for the child, not the teacher. The most appropriate placement is where the IEP can best be carried out. *The program is to be determined by the IEP, not the IEP written to fit available programs.*

The IEP must be a team product compiled by the child's teacher, school administrator, and parents (as a minimum). Parent participation in the development of an IEP is a right, not just something to be tolerated. The initial IEP meeting should also include someone from the evaluation team.

If all this sounds too complicated, we are also allowed to bring a helper with us—a trained advocate, an experienced parent, translator, or a professional who knows our child.

After the IEP is written, the most appropriate placement is found, then the IEP is implemented. The final step is to review progress. We always need to keep in mind that children change and so must IEPs.

In summary, our parental rights under PL 94-142 permit us to: (1) receive a written notice from the school for permission for tests and assessments; (2) receive a written notice before any changes are made in our child's educational program; (3) see, examine (and pay for) a copy of child's school records; (4) receive a copy of our child's final IEP; (5) discuss any serious complaints about our child's educational services; (6) obtain an impartial fair hearing when we disagree with the school on our child's program; and (7) gain an appeals procedure if we aren't satisfied with hearing results.

Attending Conferences

One of the most *challenging* aspects of being a challenged parent is the numerous conferences we have to attend. I keep reminding myself that it is my attendance at those conferences that makes me a part of the educational team.

I had been used to the traditional conference with me—feeling like Gulliver—sitting in a desk (about thirty years too small) across from the teacher. I wasn't prepared for the overwhelming formality of sitting across the table from eight professionals. I have discovered, though, that the more organized I am and the more professional I act and feel the more comfortable I become.

When I first receive notification of a school conference I start making a list of my questions and concerns. It's also a good idea to list those questions and concerns when you return your confirmation so the teacher can get any needed information before the meeting.

Ideally both parents should attend the school conferences, but when we both can't attend we go over our list of questions and concerns the evening before so we both have input.

The day of the conference I always make arrangements for care for the children and am on time for my appointment. During the conference I try to have a positive attitude towards the teacher and always start with the assumption that the teacher really has our child's best interests in mind.

We need to be honest with the teacher and give any information that will help the teacher understand our child. I share the interests, attitudes and family relationships—anything that can affect our child's academic progress.

When our adoptions were imminent I notified the children's teachers since all the excitement at home could easily affect school performances. Melissa has a sleeping problem and allergies, and I have to keep her teacher informed because they affect her daily performances.

I take notes during the conference of teacher comments and suggestions. The teacher, in turn, gives me information on our child's relationships in school, his or her interests, and academic progress.

During one of Becky's preschool conferences the teacher was shocked to discover that Becky took care of all her own toileting needs; I was equally shocked to discover she could put on her own sweater or jacket at school but played helpless at home.

When I don't understand terms the teacher uses I ask for a layperson's translation. I ask how we can help achieve the teacher's goals for our child and insure our child's school progress.

We try to maintain a balance when discussing programs and our child's educational needs—our child is legally assured an education so we don't beg; however, we try to not go overboard in the other direction and be too demanding.

I review my list and make sure I have covered all my concerns. When I feel a teacher is being unfair to my child I try to deal with it calmly, without overreacting. I also try to make a point of giving the teacher some positive affirmations.

That evening Dennis and I sit down and go over our list so that he is always a participant whether or not he can attend the meeting. Then I give him a "report" of the meeting. After our discussion we meet with each child individually.

We quickly discovered that each of our children has very different academic capabilities and we strive to recognize and respect their individuality. We can be honestly upset over the child's C because we know that child could easily get an A, yet sincerely praise another child for getting a C because we realize how hard that particular child had to work to earn that C.

Nothing can be more destructive to any fragile young

ego than telling a child who's working up to potential, "Why don't you get A's like your sister?" If our children even know each other's grades it is because *they* decided to share that information.

During our home conference we go over any information from the teacher that we feel the child needs: "You're not working hard enough," or, "You've really improved this term."

Mainstreaming Your Child

Some challenged children are totally mainstreamed into their neighborhood schools from the beginning (like our oldest children). Danny and Mark are mentally challenged and attend neighborhood schools with an aide. Toria spends half her day at the special school and half at the regular school next door. Melissa will always require a special class, however she's not isolated in a separate facility. She has contact with other children who are visually and hearing challenged, some who are only hearing challenged, and with the regular student body. The key here is what is the most *appropriate* educational setting for each individual child.

Becky attended preschool and kindergarten at the special school. The goal was always that of working towards mainstreaming her into our neighborhood school. During kindergarten she had a new evaluation done and there were many meetings and conferences. Then the decision was made by all of us that she could best benefit from being integrated into our neighborhood school for first grade.

I loved the special school. It was a safe and secure environment for Becky (and me). The children were cautious of and for each other, so injuries were rare; the facility was designed with Becky's needs in mind; the teachers were chosen and trained to work with challenged children, and no one ever made fun of Becky. Safe and secure but not the "real" world.

The special school built her self-confidence because she was always with children functioning on or below her own level. She received excellent academic training, could be screened for potential problems, and received intensive therapy. I was pleased with the decision to move her in first grade because the older children I talked with grew more apprehensive each year at the thought of leaving the security of the special school.

The first principal at our neighborhood school was very pessimistic about Becky's arrival at the school and foresaw multitudes of problems that never occurred. After five years (and seven teachers) our teacher experiences have varied from a very scared teacher, to one who kept forgetting that Becky had any challenge at all. Becky has been teased sometimes about her awkward gait and, with more children running around the playground, she has had to be more cautious about not getting knocked over. From Becky's point of view it balances out, "I miss my other friends but I like the neighborhood school best."

Successful mainstreaming (like most other important things) depends on good communication. I talked with our neighborhood principal the spring before Becky's transfer. Her teacher and therapist visited the new school, talked to the teachers, then we went, with Becky in her wheelchair, and toured the school.

A few weeks after school started (and I still do this), when I felt the teacher had a chance to get acquainted with Becky and form her own impressions, I contacted the teacher and communicated any special needs of Becky's and let the teacher know I wanted open communication. Even though I knew Becky had a legal right to be in that classroom I wanted to do everything possible to make it a less stressful situation for everyone.

While our challenged children need interaction with a

"normal" peer group they also have much to offer the other children. Other children learn to accept individual differences; recognize each one's capabilities rather than judging by his/her disabilities; understand that challenged people have the same needs and desires as non-challenged people and they learn to respect the rights of all people.[28]

The National Easter Seal Society offers some practical suggestions for when you see a new student who has a physical disability in your school:

- Say, Hi!
- Smile.
- Be yourself.
- Show friendly interest.
- Offer assistance *if asked* or if the need seems obvious (but don't overdo it or insist on it).
- Be considerate—it might take extra time for a person with a disability to get things said or done.
- Speak slowly and clearly to a person with a hearing problem.
- Give whole, unhurried attention to a person with a speech problem.
- Offer your arm to help guide a person with a visual problem—don't grasp the person's arm yourself.
- Don't move a wheelchair or crutches out of the reach of the person who uses them.

And remember . . .

- Don't be so impressed with a person's disability that you don't see the person.
- Realize that everyone has abilities, interests, and capabilities regardless of physical limitations.
- Understand that a person who has a disability is probably willing and able to help put *you* at ease.
- And finally, put yourself in the person's place. Remember that we all have handicaps; on some of us they show.[29]

The Uninvolved Parent

I have heard educators bemoan the lack of parental involvement, I have tried to get other mothers to help at a school party, I have worked months on plans for a parent meeting and had three people show up, and I've wailed about the lack of parent involvement.

But there have been other times when I've been the uninvolved parent—too tired after being up half the night with Melissa to attend an evening meeting; too involved in taking care of our empire of eight to have the time to go on field trips.

There have been times when I just didn't have the emotional strength or energy to stand up for things I knew Melissa or Becky needed. And from our experiences we have found other reasons why a parent doesn't get involved:

1. Conferences are held during school hours (8:00-3:30). With both parents so often working there are only so many times they can take off work; I feel these hours especially discriminate against and discourage father involvement.

2. Parents are not always informed of their legal rights and proper procedures.

3. Parents often don't have the skills needed to participate effectively.

4. Parents often lack self-confidence and communicate their insecurities to the educators.

5. Parents have an unbalanced perspective of their children. We need to work at and pray for a balanced perspective of our child's abilities and challenges. If we expect too little we will accuse the teachers of putting too much pressure on our child, and when our expectations are unrealistic *we* put the pressure on our child and we all end up frustrated. Eugene McDonald spoke of these expectations: "Their wish for making their child normal cannot be fulfilled regardless of how many hours of

schooling, how many sessions of therapy, how much money is spent in response to their demands."[30]

6. Overemotional reactions often become our personal handicap. I know a couple that would get very angry when they were frustrated. They were totally ineffective until they learned to control their anger.

7. Some challenged parents after years of struggling suffer from "burnout."

Prepared Parents

An effective parent is a prepared and knowledgeable parent. We need to find out what is necessary to accurately identify our child's needs and learn what types of remediation or help are appropriate for our child.

Pat urges, "Learn as much as possible about the laws that protect and guarantee your child's education, but keep in mind that no law will automatically relieve parents of their frustrations. The opportunities are there for our children now, but *we have to learn how to get them.*"

The Bay Area Coalition for the Handicapped (BACH) stresses: "The strength of our ability to advocate for our child comes from love, commitment, and *being informed.*"

Another parent urges, "I had to pay for preschool classes for my son, then fight for a public school program for him. Now we have the laws on our side, but *we need to know them so we can use them.*"

I have never been a politically oriented person, I have trouble grasping legalese, and I tend to take people and their words at face value. When Melissa was moved to an inappropriate class we went along with the administration until we saw Melissa deteriorating, then we started getting educated in a hurry.

I contacted our local legislators and got copies of all laws pertaining to special education. We contacted several parent advocacy groups and called Melissa's social worker. We literally had a crash course in Special Ed-101. Our "handicap" was that we didn't start learning to swim until after we were hurled into the water, so I now strongly encourage others to be prepared beforehand.

If we don't become knowledgeable about our child's specific challenge, educational needs, and options, *no one else will*. Many advocacy groups, parent groups, and school districts hold workshops for parents of special education children. We can share information with other parents, be observant, and read. We are on the mailing lists of several advocacy groups, parent organizations, and legislators who know we are interested in special ed. We also subscribe to a magazine for parents of challenged children (see resource list).

I'm on our Community Advisory Council for special ed and our local School Site Council. Through all these methods our education continues and we keep abreast of current issues even though we now live in a small rural community.

If we don't understand what is being done we can't be effective parents. We need to make certain we understand *everything* that is being done (or should be done) for our child. I try to learn as much of the educational terminology as I can. When I don't understand something I have it repeated, get it translated, or look it up.

In many cases if we don't ask for it our child probably won't get it, so it becomes essential that we master the fine art of being persistent without negative nagging.

There are several keys to being an effective parent:
1. Keep detailed records.
2. Be confident about your own abilities.
3. Join parent organizations.
4. Stay in close touch with your child's teacher.
5. Listen to your child.[31]

Barbara describes her method: "I write down what is said at meetings, go to the top when faced with a problem and act in a positive aggressive manner."

Pat shares the keys to effectiveness that she has learned: "Finding the correct school situation has been a long slow process and probably the most painful part of our son's challenge. Be prepared to spend time finding the appropriate class for your child. Be prepared for many meetings and school observations. Keep accurate records. Keep an open mind and listen to what the teachers are saying—they care too. Develop a good working relationship with your child's teacher. Let the teacher know about the good things that happen as well as the problems. Don't just store up problems for school meetings."

As we learn more about the whole special education process and gain skills we develop more self-confidence and effectiveness.

During our educational struggles on Melissa's behalf we discovered the importance of *home records*. BACH strongly emphasizes their importance: "At conferences, screenings, etc., it becomes obvious that you are a serious, efficient and responsible parent with all vital information at your disposal. It makes you feel more comfortable when discussing your child's education program knowing you have all the information at your fingertips in a systematic, organized and concise fashion."

We need to develop the habit of keeping written records. Jane wisely urges, "Document! Document!" If I receive a pertinent phone call I make a note of it and include the date, person calling, and purpose of the call. And when necessary I also write a letter to the caller verifying our telephone conversation.

Whenever we have important requests to make (i.e., "My child needs a new evaluation.") it is always best to write out the request. Documentation helps hold all of us accountable; educators are busy and verbal requests are easily forgotten in the rush.

Another recommendation from BACH was to write "a letter of remembrance" after all important meetings and send copies to those who attended.

When I started keeping notes from conversations and meetings I said to one administrator, "When I was working with you I never felt the need to keep records of everything. I could trust you."

He thanked me for my confidence, but replied, "Honey, I don't care how much you trust someone, or even if you're married to 'em—keep written records of everything!"

Another time I commented that I was beginning to feel slightly paranoid writing everything down. The return quip was only half in jest, "A paranoid parent is a prepared parent!" BACH recommends the following items be included in your child's home files: Keep records chronologically with the most recent on top.

- Each year list your child's:

teacher	special education teacher
school	school superintendent
principal	school board members
psychologist	special education administrator

- List the chain of command within the school system, beginning with local and ending with state and federal; include addresses and phone numbers
- Copy of Education Code—relating to handicapped children
- Copy of Title V—relating to handicapped children
- Copy of PL 94-142—and its regulations
- Copies of ALL records from your child's school—cumulative, psychological, and any other papers the school may have regarding your child
- Report cards

- Copies of test results and recommendations from outside sources
- All written (including handwritten) letters and notes to and from school personnel
- All written communication with outside professionals regarding your child's unique needs
- Dated notes on parent/teacher conferences
- Dated notes you have taken in conversations with your child's M.D. or other professionals related to your child
- Dated notes on all phone conversations with school personnel or other professionals related to your child
- List the kind, time and amount of medication being given your child at home and at school as authorized by your child's physician. Also note the Rx number as well as any changes.

I have a *profile sheet* on Melissa that I periodically update. It shows her strengths and weaknesses, the educational setting she does best in, and the type of help I believe she needs. I also attach a current vocabulary list of her signs.

This profile is obviously from a home viewpoint. Melissa is great at playing games with people. One new teacher considered Melissa "hopeless" because that's how she was acting at school. The teacher was surprised by the profile sheet and the things Melissa was capable of doing. Consequently the teacher raised her expectations of Melissa and Melissa's behavior improved.

The profile sheet is concise and easy to read and has become part of Melissa's school records.

Along with the profile sheet it may be helpful to have a personalized version of the child's medical history for teachers and other school personnel. On this sheet the medical details of our child's challenge are put in understandable language so the educators can see past the medical details to the child.

Becky's sheet would offer: (1) a simple definition of her diagnosis, emphasizing that the cerebral palsy has affected her limbs not her intellect; (2) an explanation of any equipment she uses (i.e., she must wear her braces, only uses her wheelchair when fatigued); (3) a description of any special toileting needs; (4) a description of any adaptive P.E. she requires; (5) any medication she's using; (6) any other educationally pertinent information.

Ideally we have a partnership with the school and the federal law now guarantees us our place in that partnership. The full benefit of that legislation isn't realized unless we take full advantage of opportunities the school provides us for involvement. BACH stresses, "Your success in getting as well informed as you will need to be to monitor your child's progress depends on your ability to work with the people who work with your child."

When Melissa first joined us we were in the unique position of having a teacher who knew our child better (and longer) than we did. During those early days we discovered the beauty of a close working relationship with our child's teacher.

Norma went over every sign that was used with Melissa in class so we were using the exact same signs at home. She observed Melissa during home visits and helped give me pointers on reaching Melissa. When Norma feared we were reaching our burnout level she offered to stay with Melissa so we could go out to dinner, take a nap, or concentrate on the other children.

Another teacher says, "I try to keep abreast of current legislature, issues, and services that might affect the children I teach and I share that information with parents."

The educational team concept is new for parents and professionals. Many school professionals welcome parental involvement. Others feel we are invading *their* territory.

William Cunningham, the executive director of the Association of California School Administrators, urges, "Students will only reach their full potential when parents and educators work together."[32]

One teacher sums up the ideal: "I try to serve as a resource person and be a support. I try to be available and be a good listener. I try to encourage parents to lead their own lives outside of their life with a special child. I try to be a FRIEND."

Over the years I have developed the habit of sending out numerous thank yous to people who touch my life—including teachers. I believe we all need more positive affirmation, and this is my little contribution. Along the way I discovered an extra benefit. Because I have a reputation as a "thanker" not a complainer I have established credibility, and when I have a complaint the school is more apt to listen.

BACH recommends sending letters each June to our children's teacher summarizing the year. This past year when I sent a formal thank-you letter to Melissa's teacher I also sent a copy to the Director of Special Education.

Many educators view parents as angry, pushy and overbearing, or apathetic and uncooperative. Yet many of today's programs would still be dreams if it hadn't been for some "pushy" persevering parent.

Today we have laws on our side, but some of the same old battles. What we accomplish will depend on how well we work together. We need to learn to be assertive without antagonizing and triggering hostility. We need to practice keeping calm and listening to others. We need to know our priorities so we don't waste precious time and energy on unimportant little skirmishes.

I hear parents complain, "They treat us like *we're* the handicapped"; "I'm tired of being treated like some uncooperative preschooler!"

Then I hear administrators say, "I liked it better when we gave what was needed without all these laws and paperwork—I resent being forced into providing services." One parent called that the "master-slave, client-professional, keep-'em-dependent mentality."

The authors of *The Unexpected Minority* note that professionals have less respect for parents than other professionals because parents "stand alone, not backed by government, organization, etc. so our satisfaction isn't crucial to their career."[33]

They also stress the need to change the traditional client-professional relationship previously mentioned into one of rough equality: "The average parent must be able to relate to the public school in the way that a manager relates to a consultant rather than in the way a patient relates to a doctor."[34]

In our experience we have too often found both parents and administrators wasting needed energy fighting each other rather than working together. This past year I've served as chairperson of our Community Advisory Council for Special Education and I've gained a new perspective of the administrative viewpoint. We've toured classrooms, reviewed programs and seen firsthand space, staffing, and funding problems. I no longer see things from just my parent's perspective.

Pat also recommends working with county and local school district committees for special education. "I've learned how the system works, who the people in the system are, and I've been able to bring about changes in attitudes towards parents and procedures by serving on these committees."

I have read that communication consists of good

listening, proper responses and mutual respect.[35] We used to depend on our children to keep us informed of what was going on at school, but with the noncommunicative Melissa we learned the vital importance of keeping the lines of communication open between home and school.

We have a notebook that Melissa carries back and forth between home and school. But if her teacher doesn't have time to write I have no idea why Melissa comes home in the afternoon laughing, crying, or in a tantrum. If I don't have time before school to write that Melissa was awake all night, then her teacher is puzzled by a tired, cranky child.

Several teachers stressed the importance of this communication: "It's frustrating as a teacher (and harmful to the child) when I recommend a visit to the audiologist and the parent waits six months."

"Communication is vital. I keep a notebook going and encourage phone calls."

"Don't communicate only when you have a problem or bad news."

"Build good communication, don't listen to rumors."

"Respond to communications and voice concerns when they first came up."

"Say thank you once in a while."

Working with Advocates

Today there are many different advocacy groups available. During our "problem" year we talked to legal advocates from the Center for Independent Living, Bay Area Coalition for the Handicapped, the Regional Center, Legal Aid Society, and a Deaf Advocacy group—hours of help and information at no cost to us. Whenever we ask the school district about free or low cost help, they must give us that information, but they usually won't volunteer it.

Part of our responsibility is to gather all the available information and resources we possibly can. Parents become experts at searching out hard to find services and I have often found parents knowing about resources that are unknown to the school district.

One of the groups had trained advocates that helped us obtain information and attended meetings with us. The advantage here was in having a third party who was not as emotionally involved as we were. When I was emotionally worn out or thoroughly frustrated our advocates kept up rational, intelligent communication.

Sue and her husband were easily frustrated and angered. They had a history of angry outbursts and were able to accomplish very little for their son until they worked with an advocate. The three of them went over plans together before all meetings. During meetings, when Sue or her husband got overemotional, their advocate spoke for them and eventually a new, more appropriate program was found for their son.

One group we worked with believes that an informed, prepared parent is the best advocate a child can have, and their emphasis is on training and educating parents. They hold workshops, send out newsletters, and help parents learn how to best advocate for their own child.

Eugene McDonald explains the need for advocates who are trained to help parents fight for their children's rights when fighting is necessary, and to help parents recognize when what they want is inappropriate. Dr. McDonald also sees the need for the advocate to help inform parents about what is an appropriate educational program and help parents learn to recognize and handle their personal feelings and needs which influence the habilitation of their child.[36]

Parent Groups

One of the most gratifying experiences of our challenged parenting was our contact with the parents' group at the special school Becky attended. We had a unique set of experiences to share with each other and we offered each other an invaluable support system.

Ed Hammer says, "The issue seems to be, How may parents utilize their power as persons and not risk alienating others, including professionals? Parents must first define their needs, their child's needs, and the way to achieve their needs."[37] We were able to do much of this through our interaction with other challenged parents.

Most services for our children wouldn't exist today if other parents hadn't struggled for them. Parent groups can serve many functions:

1. Share experiences
2. Define goals and strategies
3. Gain information about the children's conditions, learning approaches, and disabilities
4. Share to lessen the feelings of loneliness and isolation many of us feel
5. Maintain a balanced perspective—someone else in the group is always going through a rougher time than we are
6. Feel the political strength in numbers
7. Experience the comfort of sharing with other parents who have already passed through (and survived) our current trauma. One of the most comforting sentences in the Bible is, "And it came to pass."

Becky brought home a poem in her school newsletter that sums up the spirit of this education chapter:

UNITY

I dreamed I stood in a studio
And watched two sculptors there,
The clay they used was a young child's mind,
And they fashioned it with care.

One was a teacher, the tools he used
Were books, music and art;
One, a parent who worked with a guiding hand,
And a gentle, loving heart.
Day after day the teacher toiled,
With a touch that was deft and sure,
While the parent labored by his side
And polished and smoothed it o'er.
And when at last their task was done,
They were proud of what they had wrought
For the things they had molded into the child
Could neither be sold or bought.
And each agreed they would have failed
If he had to work alone.
For behind the teacher stood the school
And behind the parent the home.

Pulaski County Kentucky
Teacher's Directory[38]

Chapter 12

THE CHALLENGED CHURCH

Four men arrived carrying a paralyzed man on a stretcher. They couldn't get to Jesus through the crowd, so they dug through the clay roof above his head and lowered the sick man on his stretcher, right down in front of Jesus," *Mark 2:3,4.*

We once lived in a town of 130,000 people. There was still much that needed to be done for those with challenges and the situation definitely wasn't perfect, yet the secular community of that town had made a serious commitment to its challenged children and their families. There were trained medical specialists, social workers, special education programs, and organizations whose sole purpose was to help children who had vision and hearing challenges. There were varied programs available for the many levels of mentally challenged children, group homes, sheltered workshops, and advocacy groups. There were Special Olympics, telethons, numerous volunteers, and plenty of media coverage. There was legislation, regulations, and even a section of the city park with play equipment that children with orthopedic challenges could use and enjoy.

There was one small Sunday School class for challenged children in one church.

Spiritual Commitment

We have missionary conferences and our hearts are touched by the poor unreached heathen *over there.* We hold evangelistic campaigns and crusades to reach the lost *out there.* We pray earnestly for those unfortunate souls who haven't heard of Jesus and we weep for our brethren *in communist countries* who have no place of worship accessible to them.

Many Christians quote statistics proving the great need for more overseas missionaries. Many quote startling numbers of those who still haven't heard the gospel. Do you know how many challenged children were born last year? How many are in your town? Your neighborhood? *Your church?*

I am certainly not advocating that we abolish the church emphasis on missions or evangelism—in fact, the church we attend was founded as a missionary society.

I am urging that we realize that Christ's mandate to "go into all the world and preach the gospel to all creation" includes little Susie in her wheelchair who lives next door, as well as the unsaved aborigine—over there. Along with our mission and evangelism statistics we need to learn of the millions of challenged children and adults whose spiritual needs remain unmet. There is a challenged person in one out of every five families, yet one big city survey showed that only ½ of 1 percent of the churches of that city were wheelchair accessible.

Of the questionnaires I originally sent out, only one pastor knew of community resources to recommend, none had received any training in counseling challenged parents. One church had a ministry for the challenged and two churches reported having one child with a hearing challenge and one adult to sign for him.

In a day when great strides are being made in the secular community on behalf of the challenged, the church is sadly behind the times. "Until recently, the retarded and the handicapped have not been included in Sunday School planning. Scattered individual churches have courageously pioneered classes for the special child; but there is no sweeping trend to open the doors to *all* God's children."[39]

The church is known for its love and acceptance. Historically we open our arms to the unloved and unlovely. *Why then*, I keep asking myself, *the overwhelming absence of the physically and mentally challenged (and their families) from most of our churches?*

My search for answers started in the Old Testament book of Leviticus. When God set out the rules for the priesthood they were both restrictive, ". . . who have any bodily defect may not offer sacrifices to God," and inclusive, "lameness, broken bones, and pimples." Because the priesthood was to be confined to one specific family, "defects" were likely to occur. This was God's way of protecting the priesthood, but the people picked it up as an excuse for their negative reactions to anyone who was "different."

Today we are no longer under the Old Testament Law, and Matthew Henry comments on this section, "*Under the Gospel* those that labour under any such blemishes as these have reason to thank God that they are not thereby excluded." Henry continues, "Those are unworthy to be called Christians and unfit to be employed as ministers, that are *spiritually* blind, and lame, and crooked, whose sins render them scandalous and deformed" (italics added).[40]

That negative reaction towards people with physical and mental challenges continued on through history. In Roman society unwanted and/or "defective" babies were openly thrown on the town garbage heaps and left to die.

Robert Perske relates that the killing of witches during colonial days included retarded men and women. "If this is true, then one of the earliest theological views is that the retarded were viewed as 'demon controlled.' Therefore society must 'get rid of them.' "[41]

Prisons and mental hospitals were often used as convenient dumping grounds for those who were "different." Civilized people shudder at the memory of Hitler systematically destroying anyone who wasn't the perfect Aryan. (The humanists boast of the progress mankind has made, yet today we have a legal, modern equivalent of the Roman trash heap and Hitler's ovens—abortion.)

Today there is exciting new legislation guaranteeing those with challenges the right to an education, the right to work, and the right to housing. Yet most of the challenged population can't break through the architectural and attitudinal barriers to get through the church doors on Sunday morning.

After my search through history I started trying to track down modern-day attitudes. Greg Barshaw oversees the special ministries of Grace Community Church and he suggests, "In most cases the doors have been closed not because they didn't want them in the church but because they did not know how to minister to their needs."[42]

C.S. Lewis once proposed that "suffering is more of a problem for religious people than for non-religious because they have come to expect more of God."

One congregation was asked "Why did this handicap happen?" Their responses fell into five basic positions:

1. God sent the handicap as a form of punishment either for the sins of the child or the family.

2. It was a "cross" God gave someone to bear as a sign of His love.

3. It was to help the person discover and make known God's strength through his own weakness.

4. I don't know why, but "all things work together for good to those who love God."

5. God had nothing to do with it. [43]

And in *All God's Children* I found three more reasons for the church's lack of response to the challenged:

1. Fear—people are afraid of the unknown and the handicapped represent the unknown.

2. Unawareness—the Christian community is not aware of handicapped people.

3. Inexpertness—few individuals have the competencies to initiate programs for the handicapped community. [44]

Reverend Harold Wilke believes that people also challenge the challenged because they symbolize our own weakness and inability. [45]

The Accessible Congregation

Rev. Wilke states that the accessible congregation deals not just with architectural barriers but with attitudinal barriers as well. An accessible congregation:

• Sees their own psychological discomfort and attempts to deal with it

• Remembers the words of God and Jesus that sin has no casual relationship with many of these disabilities and shame is not to be connected with them

• Understands that the mission of the religious community to the world includes persons with handicaps as active agents in that mission rather than as merely recipients of that mission

- Knows from Scripture that persons with handicapping conditions have a privileged place in the kingdom
- Recognizes that although "ramps are not enough" an open attitude must move toward an open sanctuary. [46]

I have never met anyone who would deliberately add to the stress of parenting a challenged child, yet this is the result when the church ignores or sits in judgment of the challenged family. I have friends who have experienced judgmental attitudes: "If only you had enough faith— your child would be healed." "What sin of yours caused your child's condition?" "What unconfessed sin in your life is keeping God from answering your prayers for healing?"

"If the minister and congregation are not able to communicate genuine interest and concern for the family and their child along with a sense of deep respect, this feeling of being stigmatized and alienated from the religious community must be recognized as a factor contributing to the parents' distress." [47]

Jane shared: "Our pastor gave the last rites and nothing else. No provisions are made for our child at all and when we took him into church we were given such glares that we've been uncomfortable ever since." Jane simply states, "The ideal is a class that teaches God's Word to all the children—it's wrong not to."

And Gloria Hope Hawley says, "A handicapped youngster represents a hurt family. The child is a part of the family and the family should be part of the church." [48]

When we ignore and exclude the challenged child we are excluding the family.

Jesus spoke often and lovingly about the little children. He even admonished His disciples when they wanted to turn the children away. "And whoever receives one such child in My name receives Me; but whoever causes one of these little ones who believe in Me to stumble, it is better for him that a heavy millstone be hung around his neck, and that he be drowned in the depth of the sea" (Matt. 18:5,6, *NASB*).

The biblical mandate for ministering to those who have challenges is sprinkled clearly throughout the Scripture. In Luke 14, Jesus said, "Invite the poor, the cripple, the lame and the blind. Then at the resurrection of the godly, God will reward you for inviting those who can't repay you."

The other day as I was rereading the account in Mark where four men took their paralyzed friend, dug a hole in the clay roof and lowered him right into the room where Jesus was, I was struck with a new realization—with that act of friendship those with challenges were literally *dropped* into the middle of the gospel.

Christian love is exemplified by a perfect Christ loving an imperfect world. We've received it from Christ; let's share it with the challenged![49]

The Bible also warns us to not forsake our assembling together. We all need to be part of a growing, committed body of believers, but we challenged parents have an even greater need for what the church can offer.

Dr. George Paterson writes of these areas of need: The church is an important source of help; the church sustains the morale of a family that's under great stress; the care and concern of fellow believers helps feelings of guilt, grief, or resentment be resolved; religious training may help maintain hope and faith; an understanding pastor can offer invaluable support and guidance as parents work their way through a long and difficult process.[50]

Dr. Paterson also found that the family's relationship with their pastor was crucial. Even though they couldn't list specifics they reported that their pastor was with them when he was needed, that he understood and accepted them, cared about them and their child.[51]

Vicky told me that her pastor spent hours waiting with her outside the intensive care unit, and others have told me how much they were helped by just having someone listen.

Over the years our various pastors have not had all the answers, but they have helped by caring, understanding, and just being our friends. Fellowship, friendship and prayer support are lovely, welcome, and more necessary than "answers."

Why Challenged Families Stay Home

I know that despite our need for fellowship and the numerous biblical mandates for believers to gather together, on any Sunday morning many challenged families are at home. I don't present these reasons as "excuses" but to help build understanding.

● Fear: How will our child be accepted? How will people react to us?

● Self-consciousness: Many parents told me that they stay home because they can't handle the constant stares and glares. The challenged family in church is often either ignored or fussed over. We just want to be accepted like everyone else.

● Embarrassment: The embarrassment of being the center of attention (be it positive or negative) coupled with a child whose behavior is unpredictable and disruptive can keep parents "safe" at home.

● Pain: I don't like to give the impression that we have "more to bear" than others, but there are frequent times when we have just gotten a new diagnosis, or a new complication has appeared and we hurt. I have trouble during those times with shallow conversation and long for someone not to just notice my hurt and ask, "How are things?" but to really listen when I open up.

● Fatigue: At this writing Becky has an inflammation in her knee and can't walk for six weeks. My back hurts and I'm tired physically from the strain of carrying a ten-year-old up and down stairs. I am also weary from the emotional strain of entertaining her and trying to explain the unexplainable. I was up part of the night with Melissa, and Becky had to be carried to the bathroom at 4:00 A.M. I am too tired to go out to church tonight. I'm not trying to get your sympathy (well, maybe just a little!) but this is a typical time for a challenged family. When people realize our extra pressures it helps them to not "give up on us" and to continue to seek our fellowship.

• Inaccessibility: When we visit a new church it isn't just a spur of the moment impulse, but a well-thought-out exercise in logistics. Can we find a parking space near the entrance? Can we get Becky's wheelchair to the classrooms? To the sanctuary? Is the restroom wheelchair-accessible? Will the aisles accommodate her chair?

• Lack of programs: One of the biggest reasons challenged families are missing on Sunday morning is the lack of programs for our children. If a church is accessible to Becky's wheelchair she can be part of the regular Sunday School and church program—Melissa can't. Her behavior is too unpredictable and disruptive to take her into church; if there is no program for her, one of us stays home.

There is a fine line between encouraging a challenged family to attend church functions and adding another pressure. We need fellowship, even though we can't always leave the house to get it. I remember being confined to the house for long, long weeks after Becky's surgeries or the children's collective illnesses. I've ached for a phone call, someone to stop by for a cup of tea, or just a friendly note in the mail—some contact with the outside world.

I went through a time of cutting back on all responsibilities outside our home. I'm afraid there were some who didn't understand and reacted negatively to my cautiousness. However, it was a positive time for me of self-assessment and priority sorting and when I started adding things back I was very cautious to take on only what I felt the Lord was directing.

Develop Awareness

There is an Indian proverb about not judging someone until you have walked a mile in his moccasins. The Christian community as a whole needs to spend some time in the challenged family's moccasins.

A friend once stayed with our children while I attended an important school meeting. Melissa was upset at my leaving and had a gargantuan tantrum. When that was finally under control someone came to see our house (it was for sale) and Melissa kept trying to get their baby. Our friend collapsed on the sofa after the couple (and baby) left, for a few minutes of well earned rest. Becky fell and screamed hysterically at the drop of blood on her skinned knee, at which point Melissa went streaking through the house to the backyard wading pool. I returned from my meeting to a heartfelt welcome from my flustered friend who earnestly declared, "I must remember to pray for you more! I just didn't realize what it was like for you!" (I didn't have the heart to tell her that it sounded like a relatively quiet afternoon to me.)

My friend found her stay in my moccasins a bit harrowing, but she sure learned to pray for us. Our views *do* change when we really see how it is for someone else.

A pastor related that his views on the need for an accessible church changed drastically when he was confined to a wheelchair. And Buffy said, "It hurts me to say this but before my accident I wouldn't have hung around with people like me."[52]

Joni and Friends developed training programs for churches to help local congregations increase their awareness. The program sometimes includes wheelchair activities and a blindfold dinner.

How can you help develop more awareness of the

special needs of challenged families in your congregation?
● Look at your attitude.
● Look at your church building.
● Raise your fellow believers' awareness.
● Assess your congregation.
● Encourage your pastor to expound on the need to include disabled people in the life of the church.[53]

Lucille Gardner, author, lecturer, and challenged mother shares ways that her church has found to help build congregational awareness:

1. Each challenged person has his/her own prayer partner.

2. We hold socials and issue special invitations to various church leaders.

3. We integrate the children for the first part of the church service.

4. We use their talents.

5. We show slides and play tapes made in the classrooms as part of a program for other groups in the church.

This past year our church held a Handicap Awareness Sunday. Ours is a small rural congregation, yet the participation and response was beautiful. A young teen with a hearing challenge signed a song, our Becky sang, a young man who had recently lost a leg in a tractor accident shared his testimony and our church secretary told of God's sufficiency as she lives daily with myasthenia gravis.

Lucille Gardner states three necessities for the creation of a caring congregation:

1. The realization that this ministry is included in Christ's commandment to "preach the gospel to every creature"

2. The knowledge that the church can minister effectively to challenged people

3. The realization that each challenged person is an individual whom God loves.

We also need to realize that the challenged child wants the same things as any other child: friends, warmth, approval, affection, dignity, and a social outlet.

What Can I Do?

Lucille Gardner encourages, "It only takes one or two caring people to start a caring church."

At this point you are thinking, "I'm really interested in this ministry, but—I'm not experienced, I have no training. How can one person create a caring, accessible congregation? What can I do?"

Following are suggestions for that one caring person who wants to help but doesn't know how or where to start.

Visual Challenges
● Read the Bible, Christian books, Sunday School lessons aloud.
● Have your church library order Braille or talking books (see resource list).
● Tape Bible stories and Sunday School papers.

Hearing Challenges
● Learn sign language so you can communicate and/or interpret for those with hearing challenges. (Helen Keller once said, "Blindness separates us from things, but deafness separates us from people.")
● Speak distinctly to those with hearing challenges so they can lip read.
● Keep a note pad handy and communicate in writing.

Orthopedic Challenges
● Unobtrusively keep aisles clear for people using crutches or canes.
● Ask the child in a wheelchair if he/she needs help being pushed or prefers doing it him/herself.
● Seek out those with orthopedic challenges so they

don't have to try and get through the crowd to see you.
- Sit or kneel so you are on their eye level; it's hard on the neck to be always looking up at everyone.
- Don't rush them.

Mental Challenges
- Be consistent.
- Keep conversations simple without talking "down" to them.
- Expect behavior appropriate for their age.
- Offer encouragement.

General Suggestions

Give affirmation. Our eldest son had an "invisible" challenge and was constantly in hot water from his hyperactivity. When he started Sunday School he received some positive strokes and was amazed, "Somebody said I was good!"

If there are challenged children in your community that can't come to church, take the church to them. Many communities now have board and care homes, or you could take a Bible study, "Good News Club," or one-on-one discipleship to challenged homes.

Offer to help with transportation.

Be aware of challenged families in your congregation and visit, listen, send cards, and telephone.

Becky doesn't have the mobility of the other neighborhood children. They will play with her for awhile, but they soon tire of the confinement and go out. Sensitive friends in the church have her over to play, or spend the night.

Be a friend to the child. Sit with the challenged child during a service or program. This gives the child and parent a short break from each other and says to the child, "I'm proud to be your friend." Gently encourage other children to befriend the challenged child.

Take the challenged child to the park or a movie—outings are often rarities for the challenged child. Invite the child to your home for a meal or to spend the night (Melissa loves these and they are possible only with her adult friends).

Help the child cook or do crafts that can be fun with a friend—a chore with Mother. Let the child see Christ reflected in you.

Be a friend to the challenged parents. Tell them what your talents are and ask how you can best help. I've been blessed by friends whose "gifts" were as varied as ironing, baking, washing, and baby-sitting.

Listen. There are few things more unnerving than really opening up to someone about a new frustration or medical development and discovering that he/she wasn't even listening.

Give sincere compliments on the child's progress. I'm often working so hard on building better behavior patterns for Melissa that I miss seeing the very improvement I'm working for. "Strokes" for challenged parents are often rare treasures.

If the challenged parents are confined more than you are, visit them. We have friends who call, "We want to have dinner with you," and they cook it, and bring dinner to our house. It's a break for me and the fellowship is great.

Talk to your pastor and the church officers about the need to develop an aware, accessible church.

Pray with and for us.

Your church has had a stirring of awareness for the challenged children and families of your community and is interested in starting a ministry, "Of course, we want to minister to the handicapped, but . . ."

● "We're not trained."
● "It would cost too much."
● "Our congregation is too small."
● "There's no need in our area."

These are the most common excuses used to explain

why the church is lagging behind the secular world in meeting the needs of the challenged community. We need to examine each one carefully.

"We're not trained." Often providing for challenged children is a matter of common sense, not training. Becky has always been part of the regular Sunday School program, her teachers just have to do a little extra planning to make certain she can join in the activities.

When special training is required there are resources available to make such training feasible at little or no cost. We can contact a special education teacher, organizations, or a church that has an existing program (see resource list). Gloria Hope Hawley is the director of the Special Education Department of her church and she states from experience: "When Scripture sets forth a principle Christ will empower its implementation."

"It would cost too much." Ramps and extra classrooms are an expense, but can we *afford* that kind of savings?

One denomination will only issue loans for building and remodeling when provisions for the challenged are included in the plans.

"Our congregation is too small." Vicky told me about her church, "We're small—too small for a formal, special program but they accommodate Toria wherever and whenever they can."

When our small church was built, one sidewalk was extended into a wheelchair ramp and every Sunday people are wheeled over from the convalescent hospital across the street.

"There's no need in our area." I am convinced that if we advertised our accessibility on our church signs and in our newspaper ads, challenged families would flock to the church.

There are numerous joys to being a challenged parent, but there are also numerous pressures and strains.

Handivangelism, an organization in Pennsylvania, warns that "often the presence of a disabled person can cause many family tensions and problems." This is borne out by the fact that four out of five marriages that have a challenged child are failing. Clearly many families can't cope with the reality of having a challenged child.

Of the pastors I have contacted none have been trained specifically to counsel challenged parents. The need for counselors is evidenced by the fact that Joni and Friends spend much of the time in their ministry in counseling.

Many challenged families have excess medical bills, and overstrained budgets just can't cope with professional counseling fees—assuming we can find a qualified counselor!

In our years of challenged parenting I haven't felt the need (or at least I haven't recognized it) for professional psychiatric help. What I have cried for was someone to listen and pray with us. I believe that concerned lay people can be trained to help counsel in this area.

Aside from all the apparent stresses of challenged parenting are the lack of mobility and social isolation. We often do not have the freedom to come and go as we would like because we have to be available to meet the needs of our child.

The challenged family is often not able to meet new people or develop their established relationships because of their responsibilities. And others often do not make the effort to befriend the family because of their fears of the disabled person.[54]

Often parents focus on the challenge as the cause of all their difficulties. In *Shepherding God's Flock* counselors are warned to look for the following when counseling the challenged or their parents: self-pity, self-centeredness, manipulation, resentment, blame shifting, laziness and depression.

An empathetic counselor can help the challenged family get their perspective straightened out and look to Jesus.

Many challenged children can be mainstreamed into the regular church program. For those whose challenges prevent this a special education program will be needed.

Glynice's church started a special ed program *because of,* not *for,* Lisa. "This is a thank you for letting us be a part of Lisa's life." The love and compassion they have for challenged children is because of their association with Lisa.

Gloria Hope Hawley became special ed director at her church as an offshoot of paraphrasing psalms and verses for her two mentally challenged children.

And Jean Harness tells how a special ed class was started at her church, "As our daughter got older there was no appropriate place for her in the church and we felt we had only three choices: move to a church that had a special program, hire a sitter every Sunday, or have one member of the family stay home with her." Their fourth option was to start the Opportunity Class. "When Pam arrives at church she is greeted with hugs, smiles and a warm welcome. It is her place. And the Lord is her Lord."[55]

If you feel the Lord calling your church to this ministry see the resource list for details on obtaining information on starting a special ed department.

Gloria Hawley shares some of the goals of their special ed department: "For the congregation to fulfill their Scriptural responsibility and to love and accept all of God's people." The goal for the parents is that "they be completed in Jesus Christ and function as healthy members of His Body."

Mrs. Hawley shares an added blessing: "The provision of a class for every child has brought many entire families into the abundance of life."[56]

The Challenged as Blessings

Most of this chapter has dealt with what the church can do for the challenged, but we need to realize that special blessings result from following Christ's mandate to minister to *all*.

We have discovered that even when living and working with a child as multi-challenged as Melissa the rewards and blessings are abundant. God doesn't just want the gifted, brilliant, and multi-talented.

"He accepts only the perfect lamb for sacrifice, but only Jesus fulfilled that requirement. Among mankind God will use any Christian body that is committed to Him."[57]

Rev. Chuck Swindoll affirms this. "Your extra-special child will become an extra-special object lesson to others. He will be, in fact, a model of specific truths God will communicate to others."[58]

Joni Eareckson states: "I think God is going to use the handicapped community as an object lesson for the rest of the church members. He is going to use those of us who are handicapped to sensitize others to the needs of those who are hurting and teach them what it means to look past exteriors."[59]

The New Testament is full of references about the importance of each member of the body using its gift— the challenged are no exception. Gloria Hawley says, "Craig and Laura remain handicapped. God has not chosen to 'heal' them. He is pleased to use them."[60]

Those with physical challenges can usually fold bulletins and stuff envelopes. Many of the mentally challenged can set up chairs or help with yard work. For children (and adults) who are usually on the receiving end of life, being able to serve helps them gain a sense of personal worth and recognition.[61]

Isn't it amazing how God can even use inanimate objects for His own glory? Even objects that He can "speak through"—God spoke through a burning bush. Certainly if God can use inanimate, soulless objects such as these, how much more will He use real people—even with all their weaknesses and disabilities. In fact, He can even use our "inanimate objects"; wheelchairs, crutches, braces can all be a kind of testimony of how God's power shows up best in weakness. [62]

The authors of *Look at Me, Please Look at Me* describe an ugly wrapped present that held a bouquet of roses, and the caution, "Had you rejected your gift because of the ugly wrapping you would have missed the beauty of the real gift inside." [63] Many of our churches are missing that beauty.

The authors describe a group of challenged children singing "Jesus Loves the Little Children": "Here's love they can understand. A love that imposes no impossible burdens, no discriminatory restrictions, no eliminating conditions. Here is a perfect divine love, offered simply. Its only contingency an accepting heart." [64]

When we first took Becky to Sunday School she reacted like a thirsty little sponge. She brought her spastic little body and her starved-for-love little spirit and traded them for a song—"Jesus Loves Me"—and a doctrine that promised her total acceptance and eternal love. Even at three she knew a good bargain.

Ephesians 2:8 tells us, "For by grace are ye saved through faith; and that not of yourselves: it is the gift of God" (*KJV*).

"Salvation is a gift not a reward, it is something we receive, not something we perceive. It is an action of God's Spirit upon our spirits not God's mind upon our minds." [65]

Joni Eareckson was speaking to a class of mentally challenged adults. When she started talking about the new glorified body she would receive in heaven the class started listening intently. "I explained, 'I'm going to have a new body; but you guys will have new minds.' They all stood up, cheered and clapped their hands—they were thrilled!. . . Even though most of them only had the intellectual capabilities of a seven-year-old the Spirit of God had gotten through to those people."[66]

I am continually receiving reports that many secular services to the challenged are endangered by potential budget cuts and legislative changes. In the midst of today's uncertainties I am grateful that love and acceptance are available from God in limitless supply as the challenged church opens her arms and welcomes *all*.

NOTES PART IV

1. A Parent's Paraphrase of Romans 12, © 1981 by Bonnie G. Wheeler.
2. Reprinted by permission from "Parents: Do You Know the Early Warning Signs of Children with Special Needs?" published by the National Easter Seal Society, 2023 W. Ogden Ave., Chicago, IL 60612.
3. Joan McNamara and Bernard McNamara, *The Special Child Handbook* (New York: Hawthorn Books, Inc., 1977), p. 21.
4. Ibid, p. 57.
5. *The Exceptional Parent*, February 1980, p. 46.
6. McNamara, *The Special Child Handbook*, p. 93.
7. Adapted from Eugene T. McDonald, *Understand Those Feelings* (Pittsburg: Stanwix House, Inc., 1962), p. 166.
8. Anne Klingner, "The Right to Fight," *The Exceptional Parent*, December 1979, p. C 23.
9. George W. Paterson, *Helping Your Handicapped Child* (Minneapolis: Augsburg Publishing House, 1975), p. 65.
10. John Gliedman and William Roth, *The Unexpected Minority* (New York: Harcourt, Brace, Jovanovich, 1980), p. 145.
11. Ibid, p. 141.
12. Reprinted by permission from *Rehabilitation Literature*, November-December 1976, pp. 332-334. Published by the National Easter Seal Society, 2023 W. Ogden Ave., Chicago, IL 60612.
13. McNamara, *The Special Child Handbook*, p. 103.
14. Reprinted from "The Use of Drugs to Modify Behavior in Retarded Persons" by Roger D. Freeman, M.D., by permission of the Association for Retarded Citizens of the United States.
15. From an H.E.W. flyer.

16. *My Hospital Book*, by William L. Coleman (Minneapolis: Bethany House Publishers).

17. I want to thank the Bay Area Coalition for the Handicapped (BACH) for the generous use of their ideas and material in this chapter and their help and encouragement to challenged parents.

18. "Early Warning," by California Department of Education.

19. California Search and Serve, Area 4, Consortium.

20. Ibid.

21. "Practical Advice to Parents," *Closer Look*, a publication of the National Information Center for the Handicapped, 1974, p. 4.

22. Ethel Herr, *Schools: How Parents Can Make a Difference* (Chicago: Moody Press, 1981), pp. 142,143.

23. PL# 94-142, 121a14 (a) (1).

24. Margaret Daly, "Handicapped Children in the Classroom," *Better Homes and Gardens*, September 1979, p. 38.

25. *Closer Look*, Fall 1977.

26. Ibid.

27. *Closer Look*, Spring 1977, pp. 7,8.

28. "A Parents Guide to Public Education for the Handicapped," National School Public Relations Association, 1978, p. 7.

29. "When You See in Your School a New Student Who Has a Physical Disability," National Easter Seal Society.

30. Eugene McDonald, "Due Process: The Rights of Children," from a presentation delivered November 12, 1976, as part of the 1976 Annual Convention of the National Easter Seal Society.

31. Idea from "Lifeline for Janice" by Susan Thompson, *The Exceptional Parent*, October 1979, p. R 27.

32. William L. Cunningham, "Educators and Parents: Working Together We Can," ACSA Publication Department.

33. Gliedman, Roth, *The Unexpected Minority*, p. 169.

34. Ibid., p. 171.

35. Milton Seligman, *Strategies for Helping Parents of Exceptional Children* (New York: Free Press, 1979), excerpted by *The Exceptional Parent*, April 1980, p. 52.

36. McDonald, "Due Process: The Rights of Children."

37. Ed Hammer, *National Parents' Exchange*: A Newsletter for parents of deaf-blind children, December 1977, p. 2.

38. "Unity," reprinted from *Pulaski County Kentucky Teacher's Directory*; no other information is available.

39. Hawley, *Laura's Psalm*, p. 133.

40. Matthew Henry, *Commentary on the Whole Bible* (Grand Rapids: Zondervan Publishing House).

41. Robert Perske, New Directions for Parents of Persons Who Are Retarded (Nashville: Abingdon Press, 1973), p. 18.

42. Grace Community Church, *Special Ministries Syllabus*, p. 2.

43. Paterson, *Helping Your Handicapped Child*, p. 52.

44. Joni and Friends, *All God's Children* © 1981, Joni and Friends. pp. 7,8.

45. Harold Wilke, "The Ramp Is Not Enough," *The Healing Community*.

46. Ibid.

47. Paterson, *Helping Your Handicapped Child*, p. 52.

48. Hawley, *Laura's Psalm*, p. 133.

49. Thomas Cornwall and Judson Cornwall, *Please Accept Me* (Plainfield, NJ:

Logos International, 1979), p. 127.

50. Paterson, *Helping Your Handicapped Child*, p. 82.

51. Ibid.

52. Twila Knaack and Kelsey Menehan, "We Dream the Same Dreams. . . ." *Today's Christian Woman*, Fall 1981, p. 49.

53. Ibid.

54. Grace Community Church, *Special Ministries Syllabus*.

55. First Baptist Church, Santa Clara, CA.

56. Hawley, *Laura's Psalm*, p. 134.

57. John Dobbert, *If Being a Christian Is So Great Why Do I Have the Blahs?* (Ventura: Regal Books, 1980).

58. Charles Swindoll, *You and Your Child* (Nashville: Thomas Nelson, Inc., 1977), p. 134.

59. Knaack and Menehan, "We Dream the Same Dreams . . ." p. 116.

60. Hawley, *Laura's Psalm*, p. 142.

61. Joni Eareckson, "Unto the Least of These," *Christian Herald*, January 1981, p. 12.

62. Joni Eareckson, *The Caring Congregation*, Autumn 1981, p. 9.

63. Clark, J. Dahl, and L. Gonzenback, *Look at Me, Please Look at Me* (Elgin, IL: David C. Cook Publishing Co., 1973).

64. Ibid.

65. Cornwall, *Please Accept Me*.

66. Joni Eareckson, "Joni Eareckson on Her Life and Art," *First Edition*, July 1981.

Part V

CHALLENGED PARENTING—THE JOYS

Chapter 13
THE JOYS

Weeping may endure for a night, but joy cometh
in the morning, *Psalm 30:5, KJV.*

My dictionary defines joy as, "great pleasure,
delight." David Mains describes it best: "Joy is an inward
singing which cannot be silenced by outward happenings."[1]

Joy may seem a strange word to describe challenged
parenting after the heaviness of some of the preceding
material, but we are promised that joy will come. No matter what the outward happening—doctor appointments,
school meetings, lost sleep, setbacks or medical emer-
gencies—no matter what, the inward singing can bubble
forth.

Many books have been written on coping with the
stress of parenting. Few books are written on the joys—
they're usually taken for granted.

Little Johnny will roll over, sit up, walk, and graduate

right on schedule. We are proud of each event, but we also assume that those events will happen. "Comes with the territory," we say.

Not so with challenged parenting. Most of us can take very little for granted. We make no assumptions of progress; therefore, when the joys of challenged parenting appear they take on a special glow and intensity.

I have often heard that when we lose the use of one sense the sensitivity of the remaining senses increase. That same law of compensation appears in our parenting. When you are told that your child may never walk, each step becomes a miracle. When the doctors predict a child will never talk, "Ma-Ma," ceases to be the commonplace and becomes an angel song. Each time Becky brings home an honor roll report card it is a major triumph. The day Melissa signed, "I love you," was cause for celebration.

As Glynice said, "When you realize that it takes eight separate moves just to roll over you are more appreciative."

At the end of the questionnaire I asked parents to share *one* of the special joys of their challenged parenting. I was absolutely bowled over by the responses. Most responses telling of shock, trauma, and painfully learning to cope were pages long. But on that last question the joy of parenting bubbled forth—it couldn't be silenced by the outward happenings chronicled in the rest of the questionnaire.

Vicky: "Share *one* of the special joys? Boy, this is a hard one! Toria's whole life is a special joy!!"

Barbara: "We turned Danny over to the Lord at least 99 out of 100 days those first few years. Now we just see him as a *gift.*"

Barbara's seventeen-year-old daughter: "I just had to add to my mother's comments—I don't think people realize what they're missing if they can't see a retarded child as a symbol of love. My friends have been deeply touched and they see Danny as a gift from God. I wish everyone could be as loving and sensitive as Danny. Danny can only stand for love because that's all we have ever shared with him."

Pat: "The special joys are many. Michael is able to cope with a lot of difficulties which make him and us very frustrated, and yet he comes back smiling and without bitterness. He has a sense of humor, his persistence and his humility are his greatest gifts."

Glynice: ". . . oh, the joys . . . she gives so much back. What would I do without her?"

Jane: "He shares his love with others and just draws love out."

Pat D.: "It's been a joy to see our son develop from nothing and learn to read and do math. We were told he would never run and we had the joy of watching him place third in the Special Olympics."

Trina: "Parenting our daughter is like opening a gift (or many gifts) from someone who always gives just what you'll love."

Barbara: "Scott has cerebral palsy and plays Little League. His hitting range is limited (very), his running is slow motion, and his fielding is an exercise in patience. Yet each year he has been accepted and the coaches, parents, and teammates give their total support. They're excited about Scott, not because he's an all-star player, but because he has stamina, determination, a sense of humor and an all-consuming love for the challenge."

Vicky: "One of my special joys is watching the Lord feed me as I need it by bringing me new Scripture verses or reminding me of old ones. The book *Joni* was very important to us. It used to be so important that Toria walk, but after reading *Joni* I became thankful that she is alive and that became the most important thing. Toria has outlived her prognosis by eight years and our very special Scripture is from John 11:4, 'The purpose of his illness is not death, but for the glory of God. I, the Son of God, will receive glory from this situation.' "

Note
1. David Mains, *A Closer Walk with God* (Elgin, IL: David C. Cook Publishing Co., 1980), p. 118.

EDUCATION GLOSSARY

When we entered the world of special education we were once again hit with the task of learning and acquiring another new foreign language. Only this one seemed to consist of abbreviations: "Your *OH* child needs an *IEP* in the *LRE*, provided by your *LEA*."

BACH (Bay Area Coalition for the Handicapped) recommends that we always feel free to ask:

1. What do you mean by _____ ?

2. What does that mean in terms of specific action which will be taken to help my child learn?

3. How do you determine when and if such methods are appropriate to use with my child?

achievement test. A test measuring what a child has already learned.

adaptive physical education. An individual program set up for a challenged child by a credentialed adaptive P.E. teacher, focusing on remediation of specific deficit areas.

advocate. Parents, teachers, and professionals trained to provide practical information and support to parents whose children are in special education.

aphasia. The inability to express words intelligently (expressive aphasia) and/or understand the words of others (receptive aphasia).

assessment. Individually administered testing and diagnostic procedure leading to the development of a special program for a challenged child. Assessment must be done by a well-rounded team of specialists and no one test or procedure can be the sole means of making a decision about an education program. *Formal assessment* uses published, standardized tests. *Informal assessment* uses observation, interviews and teacher-made tests.

attention span. The amount of time a child can concentrate on a single task.

auditory comprehension. Being able to understand what you hear.

auditory discrimination. Being able to recognize the difference among word sounds (pop, top; cat, bat).

auditory memory. Being able to remember what you have heard.

auditory perception. Being able to receive and understand sounds.

behavioral objectives. Written, measurable learning goals.

behavior modification. The theory that since all behavior is learned, improper behavior can be unlearned. Ranges from a pat on the back for good work to confinement in a "time out room."

cognitive. Logical, analytical thinking.

communicatively handicapped (CH). Students with communicative skills disabilities: speech, language, hearing.

coordination. Fine motor: using small muscle groups (e.g. manipulation of fingers to use a pencil); gross motor: using large muscle groups (e.g. running, hopping, etc.); visual motor: ability to coordinate vision with body movements.

designated instruction and service (DIS). Services provided by specialists (not part of the school program). DIS may include, but is not limited to: language/speech assessment, audiological services, aural rehabilitation, mobility training, instruction in home or hospital, adaptive PE, coordination and/or provision of therapy, driver's training, counseling, parent education.

developmental. Sequential changes during the natural growth process.

diagnostic test. A test that measures a child's specific strengths and weaknesses.

due process. P.L. # 94-142 mandates due process safeguards in all matters relating to special education decisions. Under due process you have the right to: receive *in writing* notice of any plans or action that may change your child's school program; *written notice* if the school refuses to take action to change child's school program; *give or withhold* your consent for your child to be tested for special ed services, assessments, placement in a specific school program.

dyslexia. A person with dyslexia experiences great difficulty in sorting out words, frequently seeing them backwards or in mixed up order.

eligibility and planning team. Public school team that is responsible for admitting children to special ed programs, makes changes in individual programs and discharges students from programs.

evaluation procedure. No one test can determine a child's placement. The evaluation should include: diagnostic tests, aptitude, achievement tests, extensive talks with parents and teachers, psychological testing of behavior and functioning, observation of the child in school and play, and medical exams.

fair hearing. The educational legal procedure when there is an unsolvable disagreement between parent and school. The fair hearing can be called by either parent or school.

free appropriate public education. Every school-age child with handicaps is entitled to an education which meets his/her individual needs in a public school setting or in a private school at public expense if a public program is not available or appropriate.

handicapped child. Any child whose physical, mental, or emotional handicap makes special education necessary.

individualized educational program (IEP). As mandated by Pl # 94-142, a written statement developed by staff members and parents as a practical plan for instruction and delivery of service to students with special needs. The IEP must include: statement of the child's strengths and abilities, special problems and learning needs; annual educational goals and short-term instructional objectives; educational services; time the child will participate in regular classes; dates and time lines for specific activities; a clear statement of progress evaluation.

independent evaluation. An evaluation by qualified experts from outside the school system.

instructional objectives. Written, measurable learning goals on an IEP.

language. *Expressive*: speaking and writing; *receptive*: listening and reading.

learning handicapped (LH). Students who have significant learning or behavior disability.

least restrictive environment (LRE). Each handicapped child is to be placed in an appropriate learning environment according to his/her educational needs that is as much as possible close to that of his/her non-handicapped peers.

local educational agency (LEA). The school district a child resides in.

mainstreaming. Integration of a handicapped child into the regular classroom.

modality. A way of acquiring sensory information: auditory, visual, tactile, etc.

multi-handicapped. A child with a combination of disabilities causing severe educational problems.

occupational therapist (OT). A specialist who helps the child develop mental and physical well-being in all areas of daily living.

orthopedically handicapped (OH). When a student has a physical disability typically involving difficulty with movement and gross coordination severe enough to interfere with his/her educational performance.

perception. Process of interpreting sensory information.

perseveration. Persistent, inappropriate, repetitive behavior.

phonetics. The study of speech sounds and how they are made.

phonics. Relating the sound with the equivalent written symbol.

physically handicapped (PH). Students with physical disabilities.

physical therapy (PT). Under doctor's prescription a trained specialist works on bones, joints, muscles and nerves.

psychological evaluation. Testing to find the child's level of functioning including cognitive, perceptual/motor and emotional development.

psychomotor. The ability to voluntarily control both large and small muscles in an organized manner.

public law 94-142. The federal legislation that mandates a free appropriate public education for all children regardless of handicapping conditions.

receptive language. Receiving and understanding spoken or written communication.

related services. Services required to assist the child to benefit from special education (i.e., transportation, therapy, psychological services).

resource room. The room a mainstreamed child visits for part of the day for specialized instruction.

resource specialist. The teacher with advanced instruction in special education. This teacher works at one school in a learning center and/or the regular classroom.

rights. PL # 94-142 protects parents' rights to be fully informed and to participate in all the planning and decisions about the child's school program. Those rights include: written notice asking permission for testing, written notice before any action is taken in child's program, right to see and examine school records, a copy of the final IEP, opportunity to discuss any serious complaints, an impartial fair hearing when school and parent can't agree on the child's program, adequate appeals procedures.

school psychologist. A trained specialist who gives psychological tests, interprets results and suggests appropriate educational approaches for learning or behavioral programs.

school records. Parents may examine or receive a copy of all school records pertaining to their child. Parent may also challenge information in child's records and request it be amended.

section 504. The basic civil rights provision prohibiting discrimination against the handicapped.

self-help skills. Skills necessary for personal care and independent functioning, including eating, dressing, bathing, etc.

sensory integration. Training to help a child utilize information obtained from the senses in order to perform a complex response.

sequential. Following in time or order.

severely handicapped (SH). Students requiring intensive instruction and training.

short-term objectives. The series of intermediate steps between *now* and the accomplishment of annual goals.

special education. Defined by law as *specifically designed instruction, at no cost to parents or guardians, to meet the unique needs of a handicapped child.*

specific learning disability. Problems in academic function occurring in children with essentially normal intelligence.

speech pathologist. A specialist trained for analysis, diagnosis and therapy for speech and language.

tactile. The sense of touch.

underachiever. A child whose academic achievements are lower than one would predict, given the child's intellectual capacity.

visual handicapped. Students whose vision loss results in lowered educational performance.

visual perception. The identification, organization, and interpretation of visually received data.

MEDICAL GLOSSARY

When we were first informed that "your child has cerebral palsy" we were suddenly confronted with a whole new vocabulary: neurologist, neurosurgeon, orthopedist, orthotics . . .

I searched everywhere for simple, understandable definitions. The few definitions I could understand scared me to pieces. The others were in the foreign language of *medicalese* and I couldn't make sense of them. These early frustrations were foremost in my mind as I developed this glossary.

Included are words we are most likely to hear first; I have "translated" the definitions into layman's terms.

Admittedly, this glossary doesn't go into all the possible causes or treatments (there are just too many varied viewpoints). I just present basic definitions.

As mentioned before, the ultimate responsibility for parent education falls on us. This is merely a starting point. Use this basic glossary, and the resource list to gather information and ask question, after question, after question . . .

achondroplasia. A type of dwarfism characterized by a normal size torso and head, small face and with very short arms and legs.

acute. Short and severe.

allergist. A doctor who identifies and treats allergies, a hyper-sensitive state acquired through exposure through allergin.

amniocentesis. A process where a few drops of amniotic fluid (the bag of waters surrounding the fetus) of a pregnant woman are removed and tested for possible disease or genetic defects.

amputation. The surgical removal of a body part.

anemia. When there is a reduction in number, below normal, of red blood cells, their hemoglobin content, or both.

angiogram. An x-ray of blood vessels.

aphasia. A loss of the ability to use or understand words, spoken or written.

arthritis. Inflammation of a joint.

asthma. An episodic breathing problem, usually caused by an allergy and characterized by difficult breathing and wheezing.

atrophy. A wasting away.

audiologist. A hearing specialist.

autism. Characterized by a self-stimulating behavior that ignores external reality resulting in inadequate language, cognitive and social development.

benign. Not cancerous, not recurrent.

biofeedback. The procedure where electronic devices are used to help modify involuntary bodily functions.

biopsy. A diagnostic procedure involving removal of tissue for examination.

birth defect. An abnormality which is congenital.

brace. An appliance used to support a weakened body part.

cardiologist. A doctor who specializes in heart disease.

cataract. A clouding of the lens of the eye that affects sight.

catheter. A hollow tube used for drainage from or for introducing fluids into a cavity of the body.

cat scan. X-ray study used to diagnose soft tissue disorders of the body (especially the brain).

cerebral palsy. A group of conditions characterized by nerve and muscle impairment; caused by damage to the part of the brain that controls and coordinates muscular action.

chromosome. That part of a cell which contains genes or determines hereditary characteristics.

chronic. Long-lasting or recurring (the opposite of acute).

cleft lip, cleft palate. A congenital malformation of the lips and/or palate. Can be surgically repaired.

club foot. When the front part of the foot is in a downward angle and twisted inward.

congenital. Existing at birth.

congenital heart defect. When an infant is born with a heart abnormality in either action or structure.

congenital hip dislocation. A faulty formation of the hip socket resulting in a partially dislocated hip at birth.

convulsion. Involuntary contractions of muscles.

cystic fibrosis. A congenital disease affecting the body's secreting glands. It is characterized by thickening of mucus secretions and frequent respiratory infections.

dermatologist. A doctor who specializes in skin disorders.

diabetes mellitus. A disorder characterized by insulin deficiency.

diaphragmatic breathing exercises. Exercises to train the patient to use his diaphragm for breathing.

diplegia. Paralysis of similar parts on both sides of the body.

Down's syndrome. A type of congenital mental retardation caused by a chromosome abnormality. Severity of retardation may vary from mild to severe.

electrocardiogram (ECG/EKG). A record of the electrical current produced by heart contractions.

electroencephalogram. A record of the electrical impulses from the brain.

electromyogram. A record of responses to nerve stimulation by muscle tissue.

encephalitis. An inflammation of the brain.

endocrinologist. A doctor who specializes in metabolic disturbances.

epilepsy. Convulsions (seizures) resulting from rapid change in the function of the brain. May cause very slight physical reaction (petit mal) or loss of consciousness (grand mal).

enythroblastosis (Rh). A condition of newborns caused by an incompatibility between the mother's blood and the baby's blood.

Friedreichs ataxia. A progressive childhood disease first characterized by muscular weakness and staggering.

galactosemia. A congenital biochemical abnormality of the enzyme system; can cause mental retardation if not treated.

gastroenterologist. A doctor who specializes in the stomach and intestines.

genetic. Hereditary.

glaucoma. An eye disease with increased internal pressure and hardening of the eyeball; can result in blindness.

hearing aid. A device used to amplify sound.

hematologist. A doctor who specializes in blood diseases.

hemiplegia. Paralysis of one side of the body.

hemophilia. An inherited blood disease where one of the blood clotting factors is missing; characterized by prolonged bleeding.

hydrocephalus. When too much cerebrospinal fluid accumulates in the skull and presses on the brain. Sometimes described as water on the brain.

hyperkineses (hyperactive). Excessive amount of inappropriate activity, making it difficult for the child to attend to and complete a task, and frequently involving behavior problems.

hypoglycemia. Low blood sugar.

hypotonia, benign congenital. A muscle disease characterized by weakness at birth.

idiopathic. Of unknown or spontaneous origin.

incontinent. The inability to control bladder or bowels.

infection. The presence of disease causing organism or matter.

inflammation. When the amount of blood vessels in a certain part of the body increase and the area is painful, tender, and warm. Infection is not always present.

insulin. A pancreatic hormone used to treat diabetes.

intermittent positive pressure (IPPB). The use of a respiratory therapy unit that helps the patient in ventilating the lungs and removing bronchial secretions.

intravenous. Into the vein.

jaundice. A yellowing of the skin and eyes caused by the breakdown of pigments in the blood.

learning disabilities. When a child of normal intelligence is unable to gain basic academic skills.

Legg-perthes. Loss of bone tissue at the joint where the thigh bone meets the pelvis. Pressure must be kept off the bone during its regeneration time.

leukemia. Cancer of the white blood cells.

meningitis. An inflammation of the membranes that encase the lining of the brain and spinal cord.

mental retardation. When the intellectual process is limited; PMR—profound: IQ below 40; TMR-trainable: IQ 40-54; EMR-educable: IQ 50-69.

metabolism. A series of the body's chemical changes that maintain life.

microcephalic. An abnormally small head, usually associated with mental retardation.

muscular dystrophy. A group of diseases that cause gradual wasting of muscle with weakness and deformity.

muscle biopsy. A minor procedure where a small piece of muscle is removed and examined under a microscope.

myasthenia gravis. A debilitating muscle disease causing weakness of voluntary muscles.

neonatal. The first month of a baby's life.

nephrologist. A doctor who specializes in kidney disorders.

nephrosis. A degenerative disease of the kidney.

neurologist. A doctor who specializes in the nervous system.

neurosurgeon. A doctor who specializes in surgery involving the nervous system.

nutritionist. A specialist in the proper balanced diet.

obstetrics. The branch of medicine involving the care of pregnant women.

occupational therapy. A specialist who helps the child develop mental and physical well-being in all areas of daily living.

oncologist. A doctor who specializes in the study of tumors (cancer).

Oppenheim's disease. A congenital muscular weakness.

opthalmologist. A doctor who treats eyes.

orthopedist. A doctor who specializes in bone disorders.

orthotics. The science dealing with the development and fitting of equipment designed to help a weakened body part function.

Osgood Schlatter disease. An inflammation of the upper part of the tibia (legbone).

osteogenisis imperfecta. A hereditary condition resulting in easily fractured brittle bones.

otorhinolaryngologist (ENT). A doctor who specializes in disorders of the ears, nose and throat.

paralysis. Loss of voluntary movement of a part (or all) of the body.

pediatrician. A doctor who specializes in the treatment of infants and children.

perceptual handicap. Difficulty in interpreting the information received by the senses.

peroneal muscular atrophy. Nerve disease that causes the muscles (especially of the leg) to fail to grow.

phenyketonuria (PKU). A metabolic disease where the child can't use the protein food product phenylalanine. If untreated mental retardation may result.

physical therapist. A specialist who works with and teaches a child to use individual muscles.

poliomyelitis. A viral inflammation that attacks the brain stem and gray matter of the spinal cord.

polymyositis. An inflammatory disorder of the muscles; when accompanied by a rash it is called **dermatomyositis**.

postural drainage. A technique that helps patients get rid of respiratory secretions.

prenatal. Before birth.

prosthesis. A replacement for a missing body part.

psychiatrist. A medical doctor who specializes in the treatment of mental disorders.

psychologist. A specialist who deals with the science of mental and emotional processes.

pulmonary disease. A disease of the lungs.

pyloric stenosis. A congenital condition due to a thickened spincter muscle at the opening of the stomach into the duodenum.

quadripalegia. Paralysis of all four limbs of the body.

radiologist. A doctor who specializes in diagnosis and treatment involving radiation (x-rays).

Rh factor. See enythroblastosis.

rheumatic fever. A complication of strep throat that causes fever, inflammation of the heart, skin, and joints.

rheumatologist. A doctor who specializes in arthritis.

rubella syndrome. When rubella is contracted in the first trimester of pregnancy, fetal deformities (rubella syndrome) may occur.

scoliosis. A lateral curvature of the spine.

seizure. A sudden disease or an attack of epilepsy. A loss of control over muscle movement.

sickle cell anemia. A hereditary chronic anemia, characterized by crescent-shaped red cells; peculiar to blacks.

spina bifida. A congenital defect characterized by an opening in the lower back that exposes the contents of the spinal column.

spinal tap. A diagnostic procedure where fluid is withdrawn from the spine.

retinoblastoma. Malignant cancer of the retina of the eye.

Tay Sachs. A hereditary enzyme deficiency found mostly among Jewish people; characterized by retardation, paralysis and early death.

thalassemia. A genetic chronic anemia found mostly among Mediterranean peoples.

urologist. A doctor who specializes in the treatment of the urinary tract. .

Werdnig-Hoffman disease. A disease of the spinal cord that causes muscular deterioration.

x-ray. A diagnostic procedure to make internal images of the body by use of radiation.

RESOURCE GUIDE

As challenged parents it is our responsibility to keep informed and up to date on anything that can benefit our children. The following resources can provide us with invaluable help. Most groups publish newsletters that can keep us informed on the latest information on health, research, education, legislation and funding.

This resource list cannot possibly include all the various available resources, but it will give you a good start in building up your home resource files. For a current and complete list of groups see *The Directory of Organizations for the Handicapped in the U.S.*, from the Massachusetts Council of Organizations of the Handicapped, Harold Reemes, 41 Woodgren Road, Hyde Park, Mass. 02136.

I recommend contacting the March of Dimes and the National Easter Seal Society, asking for both general information and information on your child's specific challenge. These national organizations can give you information on groups in your area.

National Organizations

National Society for *Autistic* Children
621 Central Avenue
Albany, NY 12206

American Foundation for the *Blind*
14 West 16th Street
New York, NY 10011

Candlelighters
123 C Street Southeast
Washington, DC 20003
(for parents whose children have potentially fatal conditions)

United *Cerebral Palsy*
66 East 34th Street
New York, NY 10016

National *Cystic Fibrosis* Foundation
3379 Peachtree Road Northwest
Atlanta, GA 30326

Alexander Graham Bell Association for the *Deaf*
3417 Volta Place Northwest
Washington, DC 20007

National Association for the *Deaf*
814 Thayer Avenue
Silver Springs, MD 20970

National Association for the *Deaf-Blind*
2703 Forest Oak Circle
Norman, OK 73071

National Association for *Down's Syndrome*
628 Ashland Avenue
River Forest, IL 60305

Epilepsy Foundation of America
1828 L Street Northwest # 406
Washington, DC 20036

National *Hemophilia* Foundation
25 West 39th Street
New York, NY 10018

Association for Children with *Learning Disabilities*
2200 Brownsville Rd.
Pittsburg, PA 15210

Little People of America
P.O. Box 126
Owatonna, MN 55060

Muscular Dystrophy
Association of America
810 Seventh Avenue
New York, NY 10019

Osteogenesis Imperfecta
1231 May Court
Burlington, NC 27215

National *Paraplegia* Foundation
333 North Michigan Ave.
Chicago, IL 60601

National Association for *Retarded* Children
2709 Avenue E, East
Arlington, TX 76011

Center for *Sickle Cell Anemia*
College of Medicine
Howard University
520 W Street Northwest
Washington, DC 20001

National *Spinal Cord Injury* Foundation
369 Elliot Street
Newton Upper Falls, MA 02164

March of Dimes
1275 Mamaroneck Avenue
White Plains, NY 10605

National Easter Seal Society for Crippled Children & Adults
2023 West Ogden Avenue
Chicago, IL 60612

Religious Organizations

American Bible Society
P.O. Box 5656
Grand Central Station, NY 10163
(Scriptures)

American Brotherhood for the Blind
18440 Oxnard Street
Tarzana, CA 91356
(library service)

The Bartimaeus Review
P.O. Box 26
South Pasadena, CA 91030
(Christian Fellowship for the Blind)

Braille Circulating Library
2700 Stuart Avenue
Richmond, VA 23220
(Christian library: braille books, talking books)

Christian Fellowship for the Blind
Box 26
South Pasadena, CA 91303

Deaf Evangelism
Gospel Publishing House
1445 Boonville Avenue
Springfield, MO 65802

Deaf Missions R.R. 2
Council Bluffs, IA 51501
(catalog of Bible visuals for deaf and material about deafness)

Good News for Handicaps
6348 Jacksonville
Wichita, KS 67219
(publication: *The Challenge*)

Gospel Association for the Blind
4705 N. Federal Highway
Boca Raton, FL 33431
(gospel literature in braille, recorded sermons)

John Milton Society for the Blind
475 Riverside Drive (Rm. 832)
New York, NY 10115
(publications catalog available)

Joni and Friends
P.O. Box 3225
Woodland Hills, CA 91365
(seminars, tapes, and notebook)

First contact the headquarters of your denomination for information on ministering to the challenged. These resources include material on starting special ministries, developing curriculum, and additional resources.

Alliance
Special Ministries/Christian & Missionary Alliance
Box C
Nyack, NY 10960

Assembly of God
Ministries to the Blind/Assemblies of God
1445 Boonville Avenue
Springfield, MO 65802

Baptist
Southern Baptist Convention
127 Ninth Avenue, North
Nashville, TN 37234

Catholic
Accessibility in Religion
2445 15th Street NW # 416
Washington, DC 20009

Charismatic
Melodyland Christian Center
Joan Mallery, Director
Overcomers
P.O. Box 6000
Anaheim, CA 92806

Community
Special Ministries Dept.
Grace Community Church
P.O. Box 4338
Panorama City, CA 91412

Council of Churches
National Council of Churches
Division of Education and Ministry
475 Riverside Dr.
Rm. 706
New York, NY 10115
(resource list for ministries for people with handicaps)

Episcopal
Episcopal Conference of the Deaf
556 Zennia Land
Birmingham, AL 35215

Evangelical Free
First Evangelical Free Church of Fullerton
2301 No. Brea Blvd.
Fullerton, CA 92635

Lutheran
Ministry with the Handicapped
DLMC/DDMA
The American Lutheran Church
442 South Fifth Street
Minneapolis, MN 55415

Lutheran Church, Missouri Synod
Ministry to the Deaf
500 N. Broadway
St. Louis, MO 63102

Mennonite
Mennonite Mental Health Services
5927 Miller Street
Arvado, CO 80004

Methodist
United Methodist Center
Discipleship Resources
P.O. Box 840
Nashville, TN 37203

Presbyterian
Church Education Services
United Presbyterian Church
475 Riverside Drive
Room 1101
New York, NY 10115

Trinity United Presbyterian Church
13922 Prospect Avenue
Santa Ana, CA 92705

Accessibility Audit for Churches
The Service Center
Board of Global Ministries
United Methodist Church
7320 Reading Rd.
Cincinnati, OH 45237

The following churches and/or organizations offer packets designed to
help other churches develop a ministry to the challenged.

The Caring Congregation
139 Walworth Avenue
White Plains, NY 10606
(newsletter, book, and package on creating the caring congregation)

Grace Community Church
Special Ministries Department
P.O. Box 4338
Panorama City, CA 91412
(special ministries syllabus)

United Presbyterian Church
Education Services
475 Riverside Drive
Room 1101
New York, NY 10115
(guidelines for teaching children with handicapping conditions)

Handivangelism
237 Fairfield Avenue
Upper Darby, PA 19082
(correspondence course, camping program, curriculum development,
assists local churches in developing programs)

Joni and Friends
P.O. Box 3225
Woodland Hills, CA 91365
(offers counseling, handbook for special ministries, workshops and
seminars, Handicapped Awareness Sunday package)

The Network . . . Christian Ministries to Enable the Disabled . . . a
group of Christian Ministries and individuals with a common purpose
of seeking to enable disabled people and their families. Contact:
Edward & Judith Myers
5521 Garvin Ave.
Richmond, CA 94805

Green Pastures, Inc. (Jean Marks, Developmental Director)—Jeff
Marks, Director, 730 Cornelia Court, Mountain View, CA 94040.
Foster care for disabled children, ages infancy to 12. Also Respite
Care.

Congregational Awareness (Dorothy Clark, Director) 8 Vista Her-
mosa, Walnut Creek, CA 94596. Workshops and presentations by a
pioneer leader in teaching and including the disabled in the Christian
community. Author of *Look at Me*, and *Teach me, Please Teach Me*.

Lne' Ministry (Love Never Ends) (Richard Wardlaw, Director) P.O.
Box 125, Strathmore, CA 93267. Pastoral care, counseling and
camps-special emphasis on fellowship and recreation for parents and
their disabled youngsters.

Message in Music to the Mentally Ill (Ron Brooks, Coordinator) Ware-
house Ministries, 9844 Business Park Drive, Sacramento, CA 95827.
The gospel message presented in fresh new words and familiar
hymns, in hospitals and to individuals.

Camps

Christian Berets
(Christian camping program for challenged children)
21166 Yosemite Blvd.
Waterford, CA 95386

Directory of Camps for the Handicapped
American Camping Assn.
Bradford Wood
Marysville, IN 47141

Miscellaneous Organizations

American Printing House for the Blind
1839 Frankfort Avenue
Louisville, KY 40200

Bay Area Coalition for the Handicapped (BACH)
P.O. Box 1115
Saratoga, CA 95070
(education material)

Braille Circulating Library
2700 Stuart Avenue
Richmond, VA 23220

Children's Defense Fund
1520 New Hampshire Ave NW
Washington, DC 20036
(Special Education Guide and monthly newsletter)

Council for Exceptional Children
1920 Association Drive
Reston, VA 22091
(comprehensive publications catalog)

Gallandet College
Kendal Green, NE
Washington, DC 20002
(catalog of publications for the deaf)

Helen Keller National Center for Deaf-Blind Youth & Adults
111 Middle Neck Road
Sands Point, NY 11050

National Center for Law and the Handicapped
1235 N. Eddy Street
South Bend, IN 46617

National Information Center for the Handicapped
Box 1492
Washington, DC 20013

National Parents' Network
(National Committee for Citizens in Education)
410 Wilde Lake Village Green
Columbia, MD 21044
(Parents' rights card, newsletter, publications catalog)

Public Affairs Pamphlets
381 Park Avenue South
New York, NY 10016

Recording for the Blind
215 East 58th Street
New York, NY 10022

Teletypewriter for the Deaf
814 Thayer Avenue
Silver Springs, MO 20910
(also contact your local telephone company)

John Tracy Clinic
807 West Adams Blvd.
Los Angeles, CA 90007
(evaluation, training, and a correspondence course for parents of deaf
and deaf-blind children)

Federal Offices and Agencies

Office of Civil Rights
Department of Health, Education and Welfare
330 Independence Avenue, SW
Washington, DC 20201

Bureau of Education for the Handicapped
400 Maryland Avenue, SW
Donohoe Building
Washington, DC 20202

Closer Look
P.O. Box 19428
Washington, DC 20036
(offers comprehensive information on special education, services, and
legislation)

Crippled Children's Services
A state by state listing is available from United States Department of H.E.W.
Rockville, MD 20857
(possible source of financial help for medical expenses)

Library of Congress
Division of the Blind & Physically Handicapped
1291 Taylor St. NW
Washington, DC 20542
(free library service; over 28,000 titles of recorded books)

Also contact your local congressman or senator
US House of Representatives/US Senate
Washington, DC 20515

Athletic Organizations

American Athletic Association for the Deaf
3916 Lantern Dr.
Silver Springs, MD 20902

American Blind Bowling Association
150 N. Bellaire Ave.
Louisville, KY 40206

American Wheelchair Bowling Association
6718 Pinehearst Dr.
Evansville, IN 47711

National Inconvenienced Sportsmen's Association
3738 Walnut Ave.
Carmichael, CA 95608

National Wheelchair Athletic Association
Nassau Community College
Garden City, NY 11530

National Wheelchair Basketball Association
110 Seaton Bldg.
University of Kentucky
Lexington, KY 40506

North American Riding for the Handicapped Association
P.O. Box 100
Ashburn, VA 22011

Special Olympics Inc.
1701 K St. NW Suite 205
Washington, DC 20006

Identification Tags

Emergency Medical Identification
A.M.A.
535 N. Dearborn Street
Chicago, IL 60610

Medic-Alert Foundation
P.O. Box 1009
Turlock, CA 95380

Vital Products
Rt. 1 Box 111
Audubon, MN 56511

Magazine

The Exceptional Parent
296 Boylston Street
Boston, MA 02116
(excellent magazine with informative articles, current resources)

Clothing for Challenged Children

Betty Butler, Inc.
Box 51
Dept WD
Tenafly, NJ 07670

Clothing for the Handicapped by Adeline Hoffman
Charles C. Thomas Publisher
301-327 E. Lawrence Ave.
Springfield, IL 62717

Clothing for the Handicapped: Fashion Adaptations for Adults and
Children
Sister Kenny Institute Publications
Minneapolis, MN 55407

Clothing for Special People with Special Needs
2282 Four Oaks Grange Rd.
Eugene, OR 97405

Designs by Kay Cadell
P.O. Box 5217
Lubbock, TX 79417

Fashion Able
Box ep
Rocky Hills, NH 08553

Geri Fashions
301 E. Illinois Street
Newburg, OR 97132

I Can Do It Myself
3773 Peppertree Drive
Eugene, OR 97402

Vocational Guidance and Rehabilitation Services
2239 E. 55th Street
Cleveland, OH 22102

Miscellaneous Products

I Love You Gift Catalogue
805 N. Royal Street
Alexandria, VA 22314
(sign language T-shirts, books, etc.)

Joyce Media
8753 Shirley Avenue
P.O. Box 458
Northridge, CA 91328
(sign language books, films, etc.)

Kids on the Block
3509 M Street NW
Washington, DC 20007
(puppet programs representing various challenges, and a newsletter)

Sign Language Store
8613 Yolanda
P.O. Box 4440
Northridge, CA 91328

Special Friends
P.O. Box 1262
Lowell, MA 01853
(unique fabric toys representing various forms of special challenges)

Other good reading from Regal Books